Praise for *Rust Belt Reporter*

"I've been a fan of John Gallagher's reporting for years, but this book is a real gift, showing us what it takes to tell true stories of power and possibility. From 1970s Chicago to Detroit today, from richly staffed urban newspapers to today's local news patchwork, *Rust Belt Reporter* is an intimate revelation of how the quiet glory of journalism is intertwined with the fate of our cities—and ourselves."

—Anna Clark, author of *The Poisoned City: Flint's Water and the American Urban Tragedy*

"A master of explanatory journalism, Gallagher now takes on the subject of his own life and career. He's given us several books in one, including a primer on his craft, a reflection on the newspaper business, and a summation of four decades chronicling the declines and revival of his adopted city of Detroit."

—Rip Rapson, Kresge Foundation President and CEO

"A poignant tribute to Detroit and the power of resolute reporting. Gallagher is one of the few writers who has chronicled the condition of America's older, industrial communities in a way that inspires leaders to act. He sure inspired me."

—Congressman Dan Kildee

"Take a ride with Rust Belt reporter John Gallagher.

"Gallagher hopped aboard the *Detroit Free Press* in 1987 for the ride up. With a seat as a business reporter at a major news chain, he clickety-clacked his way to the top. He covered mega-corporations, a storied city, society, architecture, and the transformation of suburbs and cities, which he prefers.

"As his ride crested, a wheel came off. Then another. The tracks groaned. The ascent stalled. Decline began.

"Gallagher reported on car companies begging for federal bailouts while the city lurched toward bankruptcy, residents moved away, and the majority Black population suffered. The mayor went to prison; the city went bust; the economy tanked; Detroit's newspapers took a strike. They lost readers and advertisers. Publishers pinched profits from their dying business model.

"As the newspapers pushed some staffers off the tracks and others jumped, Gallagher stayed. He climbed to the front car where the view for stories is best.

"We overlapped at the *Free Press* for more than twenty years. Gallagher was quietly amazing. Sometimes, including a Sunday when he was at home, I once asked Gallagher how he knew what he knew or learned to do what he did. In this memoir, he spills his secrets and tells what he saw."

—Joe Grimm, *Detroit Free Press* reporter (1983–2008) and Michigan State University emeritus professor of journalism

RUST BELT REPORTER

Great Lakes Books

A complete listing of the books in this series can
be found online at wsupress.wayne.edu.

Editor
Thomas Klug
Sterling Heights, Michigan

RUST BELT REPORTER

A Memoir

John Gallagher

Foreword by Stephen Henderson

WAYNE STATE UNIVERSITY PRESS
DETROIT

ISBN 9780814351482 (hardcover)
ISBN 9780814351499 (e-book)

Library of Congress Control Number: 2024934526

Jacket design by Brad Norr Design.

Publication of this book was made possible through the generosity of the Friends of the Great Lakes Books Series Fund.

Wayne State University Press rests on Waawiyaataanong, also referred to as Detroit, the ancestral and contemporary homeland of the Three Fires Confederacy. These sovereign lands were granted by the Ojibwe, Odawa, Potawatomi, and Wyandot Nations, in 1807, through the Treaty of Detroit. Wayne State University Press affirms Indigenous sovereignty and honors all tribes with a connection to Detroit. With our Native neighbors, the press works to advance educational equity and promote a better future for the earth and all people.

Wayne State University Press
Leonard N. Simons Building
4809 Woodward Avenue
Detroit, Michigan 48201-1309

Visit us online at wsupress.wayne.edu.

To Sheu-Jane, always
and
To my newspaper friends down the years
who helped see me through

You live in Detroit and also work in the newspaper industry. Are you a glutton for punishment?

—Stephen Colbert to Stephen Henderson on *The Colbert Report*

Contents

Foreword

The end of the first decade of this century and the early teens were pretty rough times in Detroit.

A major scandal engulfed the administration of a popular young mayor who seemed destined for national greatness. The auto companies that sustained every nook and cranny of the local economy for a century hit the skids hard, with two of them having to declare bankruptcy. And the city itself, after years of gaming its own finances and borrowing a staggering sum just to keep operations going, declared the largest municipal bankruptcy in American history.

These were existential crises for the city—complex and complicated troubles that threatened destabilization of Detroit's present and doom for its future.

They were also clarion calls to local media. These kinds of difficulties are what modern newsrooms had been designed to penetrate and make sense of. Newsrooms were full of reporters who had the experience and expertise to help guide the community through with depth and understanding about what was happening. And Detroit journalism did its job. These crises were not just reported by the local newspapers. They were dissected, and explained, and contextualized in powerful and meaningful ways by two dailies, the *Free Press* and the *News*, which had made sense of the world to readers for as long as anyone could remember.

This memoir crescendos around that period of journalism in Detroit, a time that saw the city tested in ways it could not have imagined but also saw local journalism shine in its ability to inform, explain, and advocate. John Gallagher, a longtime business reporter for the *Detroit Free Press*, was at the center of coverage for all of those huge stories. Count the bylines—there are too many to mention. And measure the impact—Gallagher's work during this period made the *Free Press* stand out.

Inspiring as it is, that success brings into relief a more contemporary question. If any of those stories were to unfold in Detroit today, would they be covered in the same depth? Would they be covered with the same relentless pursuit? Could they be covered with the weight—again, of experience and expertise and understanding—that was abundant in the local newsrooms a decade or more ago? Anyone who has been paying attention would have to say no.

Deep cuts in every kind of journalistic resource have reshaped the dynamics at the daily newspapers in Detroit, just as they have in cities all over America. And while there is an exciting crop of small, nonprofit newsrooms growing in the city, none has the reach or depth of the traditional newsrooms that we've seen disappear. Gallagher, in this memoir, marks in vivid detail and narrative the pivot point that his generation represents in this transition.

That turn also punctuates my own career in news, and much as it is for Gallagher, it's a point of profound sadness and angst for me. But Gallagher manages a remarkable balance in this work. There is no doubt about his laments—about the losses and dismantling of the news business, and the effect that might have on Detroit, the city where he spent the bulk of his career. But he also celebrates, with joy and admiration and satisfaction, the time he had in a healthier news industry, growing up through ever bigger newsrooms and editorial challenges, and grappling ultimately with the series of crises that unfolded in Detroit in the early part of the twenty-first century.

This is an important undertaking for its personal arc. Gallagher has had a remarkable career and is not just a respected voice regarding the victories and challenges facing Detroit. He is a pillar of knowledge and understanding, a journalist with a broad and deep array of sources and experiences and memories who cannot be left aside of any serious conversation about the city's fortunes. But it is also a critical work for its documentation of the overall sweep of change that is overtaking the news business.

Gallagher's early career, in the 1970s, unfolds as much of the press, particularly in cities like Chicago, where he is a young reporter, is enjoying a heyday of influence and power. The industry's business model is producing millions that are used, in large part, to provide opportunities for young aspirants like Gallagher. And the newsrooms have not just healthy numbers of journalists but reporters whose longtime work had elevated them to a degree of skill and insight that served readers wonderfully. This also made newsrooms dazzling

places for younger reporters like Gallagher. But by the end of Gallagher's time in newsrooms, papers like the *Free Press* are just holding
on, buffeted by round after round of staff and product reductions,
raising more questions than answers about the future of journalism, and democracy.

I spend a lot of time these days with younger journalists in Detroit,
people who are now the age Gallagher was when he was cutting his
teeth on stories in Chicago. One big difference for them is the result
of what Gallagher chronicles in his memoir, the disassembling of
major newsrooms in cities like Detroit. The good news is that a new,
vibrant collection of small, mostly nonprofit newsrooms has sprung
up in the last decade or so, and they are trying mightily to fill the
chasm that has opened in local news coverage.

I founded one of those newsrooms, BridgeDetroit, and our
reporters are dedicated to the same things Gallagher was when he
was their age. But I worry, a lot, that these young reporters and new
organizations are missing out on the kind of mentorship and sys-
temic learning that the old, big newsrooms offered. Yes, those newsrooms were too male, and too white, and their sensibilities reflected
that make-up. The young journalists I work with today are a much
more diverse group, and see journalism as a path to championing more
inclusion, both in staffing and in coverage. Those are wonderful goals.
They are being realized slowly, but meaningfully. But they are forg-
ing a path that is much more dimly lit, and less paved, than the one
Gallagher had. They are doing it without the infrastructure the news
business once had.

What I wish for them, though, is that they might travel the same
arc that Gallagher so artfully illustrates in this memoir. A life of story-
telling, punctuated by growth, and learning, and influence, and joy.

It will be tougher to come by, given the circumstances.

Here, Gallagher shows the value of perseverance, and belief.

Stephen Henderson

1
Ashes to Ashes

Here's one difference between a young reporter and an old one.

It was a humid August night in 1974, getting late, and I was finishing my shift at the City News Bureau of Chicago. City News was the oldest of old-school newsrooms, something out of the 1940s, down to the ancient switchboard and the teletype machine tat-tat-tatting away around the clock and the police and fire scanners keeping up their low-level chatter. Just as I was walking out, no doubt headed for a beer at Billy Goat's, the scanner came alive with a report of a fire high up in the newly opened Standard Oil skyscraper on Michigan Avenue. The gleaming white tower was the latest edition to the skyline of Chicago's Magnificent Mile. This was just when the disaster movie *The Towering Inferno* about a skyscraper fire had been filling theaters. A fire at the Standard Oil building would be news. My editor told me to drive by on my way home in case there was something to it. But moments later, the scanner all but screamed as the first responder on the scene called for a lot more help: *"Emergency! Gimme a box!"* A box was the first level of fire response; the fire would shortly bring multiple extra alarms.

I had been a reporter for less than eight months. After finishing college I had drifted somewhat in search of a life, taking a few graduate classes that led nowhere, spending several months in a deeply demoralizing business office. Then I worked half a year as a shipping clerk in a book warehouse while I applied all over Chicagoland for newspaper jobs. I had written for my school papers and relished the immediacy and intensity of daily journalism, the feeling of being where things were happening. When the call and offer finally came from City News, I found the job almost more than I bargained for—months of long hours, abysmal pay, getting yelled at by homicide detectives for getting in the way, and suffering never-ending criticism from my editors. But I loved being a reporter, loved seeing so much more of life than I was used to and putting it all down on the page. My desire to succeed in my new life remained at high pitch as I rushed into the lobby of the Standard Oil skyscraper that summer night.

The fire was on the tower's twenty-fifth floor. Joe Cummings, a radio reporter for the all-news station WBBM, a big bluff journalist who took the time to talk to us City News "kids," was already on the scene in the lobby when I got there. A dozen or so firefighters in full gear crowded into one elevator to ride up to the twenty-fourth floor, where they would get off and climb the stairs to twenty-five to fight the blaze. A few more stepped into the next car and Joe and I got in with them. Just as the door started closing, a building security office looked suspiciously at us—two guys in civilian clothes instead of fire-fighting gear—and asked who we were. Joe answered "police" and then added, in a much lower voice, "reporter." We weren't stopped.

The elevator doors opened on twenty-four to an office scene of desks and cubicles in an open floor plan. A dusky haze filtered down from the fire, and water dripped through the ceiling—evidence of both the blaze and the firefighting already underway one floor above us. Some of the firefighters were moving desks away from the drip-ping rivulets. Reasoning that this office used the same phone system we did at City News, I picked up a receiver, dialed 9, got an outside line, and called my office. When I told my editor where I was, he sounded, well, alarmed. "Take it easy!" he told me.

Soon the firefighters had gotten water on the blaze and had it under control. As other reporters joined Joe and me, we climbed the stairs up to the twenty-fifth floor. I was shocked to see what fire can do; the office floor was now a gutted, blackened ruin. All was in darkness but for the emergency lighting piercing the gloom. We gathered around the fire chief, our feet wet from the hoses. The chief briefed us on what he knew, but the thing I remember best is the young firefighter I interviewed among the wreckage, his face covered with soot, blank with exhaustion, who had been first on the scene. The fire, he said, had been "hotter'n a bitch."

Times change, and with it how a reporter would cover a blaze like that. Maybe it was the business that changed, as phalanxes of marketing and p.r. staffs learned to insert themselves between reporters and the story. Or maybe I just grew older and more cautious. But it probably wasn't another five years before I wouldn't dream of riding an elevator up to one floor below an extra-alarm fire. It was Youth that did that—Youth and my eagerness to be a "real" reporter, like some of the legends I'd been weaned on. Sheer animal spirits will drive a twenty-four-year-old to do stunts wiser folks don't do. By the age of forty or fifty, deep into my career, I suspect I might have been among the media waiting in the lobby for the fire chief to come down to brief us.

Make no mistake, I'm not regretting the maturing process I went through in years to come. I was strictly a novice in those City News years, midtwenties and as raw as they come. I would grow into a solid journalist, proud of my expertise in urban affairs and economics, writing books, winning awards, possessed of an ability to interview anyone and to turn out good copy on tight deadlines. I certainly wouldn't trade what I became to stand once more in the shoes of the callow lad I was the night of that fire.

But I do sometimes look back with fondness and perhaps just a twinge of regret at my lost City News days. That youthful glee—for I was ridiculously happy with my story and my little adventure—that glee, once gone, never quite returns.

* * *

There's one other way that young reporter differed from the mature journalist I became. That kid could still look forward to a traditional newspaper career, where the highest goal was getting a blockbuster on the Sunday front page of a major newspaper, and the highest career aspiration was to become a columnist. No one had ever heard of the internet then, or digital platforms, or X and Instagram. We had barely heard of computers; we were still using manual typewriters and carbon paper at City News. The idea that a digital startup like Facebook, whose founder, Mark Zuckerberg, *wasn't even born yet* on the night of the fire, could destroy the print newspaper industry—that the hundreds of staffers at mighty papers like the *Chicago Tribune* could dwindle to a pitiful few, that newspapers' economic model would collapse and many thousands of journalists lose their livelihoods—such an idea would have struck all of us at City News as bad science fiction.

The young reporter who flew to the scene of the fire knew, with a moral certainty that ought to frighten anyone who feels this way, that his industry was secure, that the outlook for journalism was bright, unchanging, and solid. When he rode the elevator to the twenty-fourth floor he had no inkling that his world of newspapering would also one day burn to ashes.

2

Beginnings

If you plan to follow along with my memoir to the end, you probably want to know more about your traveling companion.

And so:

I was born at nearly the midpoint of the twentieth century, in November 1949, in the New York City borough of Queens. My parents, Helen and John, were both New Yorkers, Dad growing up in Brooklyn and Mom in the Forest Hills area of Queens, both sides of the family not more than a couple of generations off the immigrant boats. My folks met just after World War II when Dad came home from the Army and rejoined General Motors in a Manhattan office where Mom worked clerical. They married just under a year later and had five children. Today that size brood sounds like a home-schooling Mormon family in the rural West but of course it was quite common for us early Baby Boomers. It made for a crowded household, matched with the multitude of aunts and uncles and cousins on both sides. I've often told my wife that my unbreakable lifelong habit of showing up as early as possible for planes, movies, and dinners stems from growing up in a big family, where being late was to miss out. (She smiles indulgently at this.)

What we know today with twenty-first-century hindsight is the importance for children of having both parents present in a nurturing relationship, even if that relationship includes all the usual spats and storms. My parents were married for seventy-two years, then died four weeks apart. I accept now that any success I've had finds its origin in growing up in a stable, two-parent household where education, obedience, and duty were emphasized.

Some of my earliest memories are of my mother reading to me, an inestimable gift. From the earliest age I absorbed books, couldn't do without them. Childhood stuff at first, Hardy Boys, *Treasure Island*, and Jules Verne, before moving in my teens to the meat of Hemingway and, later, Faulkner. From the beginning I had an absorbing fondness for history books, the pageantry and narratives, and still do. Once, when I was about age eight, my older sister missed a few days of school and asked me to collect some of her textbooks from her class to study at home. She hadn't asked for her history text, but I took it anyway—two grade levels above my own—just to read it myself.

It was an Irish Catholic family at a time when the tangles and briars of the immigrant church still clung to our lives, so when my father's job took us to suburban New Jersey my parents sent us to St. John the Apostle School in Clark Township. I gladly pay tribute to the nuns who devoted their lives to educating me and their other charges, but I could have done with fewer of the never-ending messages of sin and redemption we heard year after year, the unrelenting condemnation of anything to do with sex, which at our age in grade school mostly fell into the category of "impure thoughts," of which I had plenty. So many others have written about the joys and absurdities of a Catholic school education at that time that I don't need to belabor them here. (Listen, if you like, to George Carlin's brilliant "I Used to Be Irish Catholic" or read Jane Trahey's warm-hearted *Life with Mother Superior*.) But the notion that all the boys and girls shrugged off the fire-and-brimstone stuff to emerge unmarked is probably wrong. Certainly more than a few of us internalized the message of inescapable guilt. And I suspect it stayed with us, in ways unforeseen. Decades later, when I became known as a prolific newspaper writer, able to almost shake stories out of my sleeve; when one editor called me the hardest-working man in Detroit journalism and another colleague dubbed me a writing machine for my output— I sometimes thought, hey, it's not hard. All you need to do is attend Catholic school in the '50s, absorb all of that *I-am-not-worthy* breast beating, and then you may spend the rest of your life working hard to prove that perhaps you are worthy, after all.

My father's job with General Motors (GM for, I suppose, "Get Moving") took the family first into New Jersey then across the country to Portland, Oregon, and then to suburban Chicago. Those head-spinning moves usually came at a bad time for one or another of us; I still remember my older sister's outraged tears and my own hollow resentment at having to give up the familiar to be thrown into the strange and new. I've long since accepted the trade-off, a balance of gaining wider experience of the world at the cost of an occasional uprooting. (I would find that trade-off again, later, in journalism.) And life proceeded apace. One afternoon in high school in Portland, looking for a new activity, I walked into a recruiting meeting for the school newspaper. To say I took to it would understate it by orders of magnitude. Interviewing people, shaping words and paragraphs, laying out the pages with different type faces and photos, all of it absorbed me in ways nothing else had. Not for nothing did one of my favorite teachers write in my yearbook that he thought I was happy only in a newsroom. I was young, and it took me some years before I realized how right he'd been.

I attended college at DePaul University in Chicago, majoring in my first love, history (there being no journalism degree there at the time). This of course was during the Vietnam War, and like all the other young men my age my birthdate went into the first draft lottery, the specter of which would warp so many lives and plans. My number came up 282 out of 366 days (including leap year babies), and that was far beyond what the military drafted that year. So I never had to go fight in a foreign war, which of course brought me a full measure of relief along with the guilt for not sharing the sacrifices of so many others, no matter how misguided the war itself.

DePaul was and is a first-rate school, but I suspect my best education came from absorbing the Chicago scene—its history, architecture, its bumptious politics, its lively newspaper wars. Some of the books I read then—I recall Theodore Dreiser's *The Titan* about a corrupt Chicago financier and fixer—sharpened my focus on the guts and wiring of great cities. Later in the '70s Robert Caro's landmark *The Power Broker* became a bible for me, its examination of how Robert Moses wielded unchecked power for decades in New York City the best book ever written about American cities, urban politics, and in many ways urban journalism, too; the depth of Caro's research and the clarity of his prose became a career-long model for me. Much later, my newspaper job in Detroit not only gave me a catbird seat over America's greatest urban story—the rise, fall, and rise again of a great America city—but also gave me the freedom and wherewithal to visit and write about cities everywhere, from New York to Los Angeles, Toronto to Vancouver, Paris to Prague and with a memorable stop (as we'll see later) in Berlin the same week the Berlin Wall opened. I came not only to reside in cities but to know them, to study their innards, their human infrastructure and their built environment, their conflicts and their civilities (yes, civilities, since cities at their best are the most humane places I know). My fascination with how cities work, how they thrive or fail, sent me looking for what works and what doesn't in every city's quest for renewal, and this became my career-long endeavor. But the seed of my interest, the embryo, the first kindling of my passion for cities, first stirred in me during my youthful Chicago years, when even riding the El trains or walking the streets in disparate neighborhoods gave me the best start on an education in urban affairs I could ever get. I owe a lot to many people and places for my newspaper success and for the books I would write, but it all started in that city on the lake. And for that, Chicago, I'm forever grateful.

But that insight into a career direction came later. When I graduated from DePaul in the early '70s, I yet had formed no plan for my life, nor understood what I might be good at. I toyed with graduate school, took a couple courses toward a teaching career, but neither stuck. I was in a hurry to get somewhere, but the goal remained hidden from me. To avoid just vegetating in my parents' spare room I took a business office job with a manufacturing firm in the western suburbs. I spent a dispiriting year dragging myself to the office each morning to do work that brought no joy, feeling as alienated from my best self as I've ever been. It was a miserable time.

Then I recalled those early high school days at the school paper. I quit the office job, got some work loading shipments in a religious book warehouse (stealing time during breaks to read their wares, theological books about the Dead Sea Scrolls or the Virgin Birth), and sent out résumés to newspapers. Someone mentioned to me an outfit called the City News Bureau of Chicago, which hired newbies to staff the police precincts and municipal offices to send news to the major dailies and broadcast outlets in Chicago. I learned it was a famed starting ground for journalists and writers; among its alumni were columnist Mike Royko, investigative reporter Sy Hersh, novelist Kurt Vonnegut, artist Claes Oldenburg. I traveled the commuter train into the city one morning and interviewed with Larry Mulay, chief executive of City News for decades, who enthused about the training, told me to cut my hair shorter (it was longish then), and said they'd be in touch. I called every month to check, always hearing not yet, not yet, until the day when he told me that if I came in Monday morning, I'd have a job.

I've often reflected that only in youth is the gap so wide between the passion and desire burning within us and the paucity of ways we can put it to use. I was two years past college when the job offer came from City News, and those two years had done little to fulfill me. I was unmarried, didn't have much money, worst of all had felt a lack of direction that, if not corrected, could have left me embittered and chasing all the wrong things. But now I saw a new beginning with the job offer from City News. Even before I started work there, I had mentally and emotionally committed myself to my role as a journalist. There was only forward. That was my frame of mind on the cold Chicago morning, January 21, 1974, when I nervously walked into the City News Bureau office in Chicago's West Loop to begin my new life.

3

Chicago Reporter

I asked the chief editor and proprietor (Mr. Goodman, I will call him, since it describes him as well as any name could do) for some instructions with regard to my duties, and he told me to go all over town and ask all sorts of people all sorts of questions, make notes of the information gained, and write them out for publication.

—Mark Twain, *Roughing It*

Ben Hecht, the coauthor of the newspaper play *The Front Page*, began his career working for the old *Chicago Daily News* in the early twentieth century. He later wrote that journalism requires little from its practitioners but enthusiasm. That I had, and that I needed, on that first day (and all subsequent days) at the City News Bureau. CNB offered the sort of introduction to journalism that I don't think exists anymore in the trade. I hesitate to call it "training" since there were no instructional sessions, no cozy meeting with my new colleagues, no handouts or tutorials to mull over. On that first morning, Paul Zimbrakos, the longtime chief editor, assigned me to another police reporter (who herself had been on the job mere weeks) and we immediately left for a police precinct on the near north side. There we spent hours on our feet at the precinct's front counter working the phones to check out the list of unnatural deaths the office had given us—murders, accidents, unknown causes—while staying out from underfoot of the cops who came and went throughout the day. That first day my only memorable story was a suicide of a retired firefighter who had become discouraged and desperate by the onset of blindness. It was a suitably grim introduction to the realities of police reporting. By the end of a very long day, I was shell-shocked at the brutal pace and the unrelenting demands of my editors. But

I came back the next day, when I was sent out on my own (one day of shadowing another newbie reporter was all the training we got at CNB), and all the days that followed.

It seems I did well, for after three weeks of dayside work I was given what was considered a key assignment staffing the press room at police headquarters, then at Eleventh and State Street, on the midnight shift, where I was to keep tabs on the entire city as the only City News kid working the overnight hours. I was surprised, since I'd been told one got the overnight beat only after months on the job, but Wayne Klatt, our editor in the evenings, told me I'd had the best debut of any new reporter in a long time. *That* surprised me, too, but perhaps my Catholic school training and its accompanying guilt made me doubt how well I was doing.

The press room at police headquarters was staffed by old-timers from the newspapers, including local legends like Walt Spirko of the *Sun-Times* and Joe Morang of the *Tribune*. Spirko had covered the infamous St. Valentine's Day Massacre in 1929 and more than forty years later he could still regale young reporters with his tales. Joe Morang, to get stories over the phone, used the old Chicago press technique, now thankfully long out of date, of pretending to be police himself. At his direction I tried that once or twice myself in those first weeks, hated doing it, felt guilty, realized it was silly because I got just as much just by saying who I really was, and never did it again.

Perhaps the greatest thing about City News is that we got paid (not much, for sure) to make our mistakes on the job. For me, that started on my first day, when I showed up that first morning and presumed wrongly that the office would provide the pens, notebooks, and other stuff we'd need. I didn't count on how low-budget City News could be. When I asked Zimbrakos for a pen he scolded me for not having one. "That's terrible!" he said, shaking his head, as if wondering if I would make it as a reporter. No wonder that for decades afterward I never left home without two or three pens in my pockets.

A few weeks after that first day at City News, I was covering the midnight shift when I heard that a policewoman had made an arrest—the first since female officers had been assigned to patrol duty on the Chicago force. I called the station and spoke with her and wrote it up, but in my inexperience, I didn't get anything resembling a good quote from her. My report, called in to a rewrite man on the overnight desk, was factual but dull. I was sleeping soundly later that morning after my shift when Zimbrakos called to ask for more color for my story. Women cops on the street were a big deal, he reminded me, and to bring a story to life it was always "quotes, quotes, quotes." I remembered that the officer had told me with a chuckle that the teens she had nabbed had spoken "a few naughty words," but that was about all I could add. Need I add that I have listened for the telling quote ever since?

A tragic story drilled home another lesson. I was on a midnight shift at City News when two Chicago cops approached a suspect in a bar and the suspect pulled a handgun and shot both officers dead. The manhunt was immediate and massive. I drove to the operations center where dozens of detectives had gathered, some in coats and ties, others in grungy undercover clothes, all armed with one or two handguns holstered at their waists or in their armpits. I had never seen so much firepower. At one point a tip on the suspect's where-abouts came in and the cops raced out of the station to get to the scene. I wasn't sure at first what was happening and didn't have the presence of mind to jump in one of the cars and beg to be taken along. Instead I ran to the pay phone in the station and breathlessly called my overnight editor that something *really, really big* was hap-pening. But where were they going, he asked? I don't know, I said, but they really ran out of here. . . . At this point he stopped me. "Part of the *game*," he scolded, was to get some hard information before I called the desk. Sheepishly I set about trying to get some useful facts. As it turns out the tip had been false; the gunman had fled north to Milwaukee where police there shot and killed him. But that night taught me to keep my cool when covering a dramatic breaking event. I admit I learned the lesson only after losing it a few times in my early days.

City News paid very little; my starting salary was $125 week with no overtime pay for all the extra hours we put in (fifty- and sixty-hour weeks were common). On that pay I could afford a basement apartment in the Rogers Park district on the north side that was so cold in Chicago's frigid winter nights that, coming home from a shift in the predawn hours, I would turn on the oven in the kitchen and sit near it playing solitaire until the radiators started to hiss and bang with the first warmth provided by the landlord; then I'd go to bed fully dressed, socks, jeans, shirt, and all. I recall this only to bring out how sold I was on this career. With my college degree I could have found something with better pay and better hours. But from that first long day at City News I was a journalist and that was that. If there's such a thing as a calling, or at least a career one is best suited for, I had found myself as a reporter. As Yoda says in the *Star Wars* films just coming out then, "Do or do not. There is no try." It would take more than a cold, drafty basement dwelling to make me give up my life's work. I doubt now whether anything could have.

The technology at my first job at City News was decidedly old school. The owners of the bureau, the major local papers, invested as little as possible in the operation, including in the meager salaries for reporters. In the office in Chicago's West Loop we made our telephone calls not with a modern desk phone with flashing buttons and multiple lines, but a truly ancient device resembling a switchboard from a 1940s movie. We transmitted our stories to our clients, which were the major papers and broadcast outlets in town, via a teletype machine, the ratchety-clack kind you see in old movies. After a story was written (using manual typewriters and carbon paper), one of us (and I had to train on this as part of my duties) typed in the story on the teletype, producing a long, thin ticker-tape strip that we fed into a sender. On the receiving end in newsrooms around the city, the story would clickety-clack print on paper. Copy kids or editors would rip off the stories and, if deemed interesting, give it to one of their own people to follow up. On our broadcast side, where we wrote summaries of the news for our radio and TV clients, the stations would often just "rip and read," with no further reporting or editing of their own.

One drawback of these old teletype machines is that you couldn't see what you were typing as you went; all you saw was the pale yellow ticker tape slowly feeding out with all the holes punched in it. Only when you fed that into the transmitter did you see your story typing out on paper just as the client recipients did, at the same time, on their end. Once, through a freakishly inept fumble-fingered mistake on my part, instead of typing "Firemen were battling an extra-alarm fire" it came out "Firemen were balling a. . . ." I hastened to send a correction, but the mistake drew guffaws and snorts of derision in newsrooms around the city.

Eventually after many months on the midnight shift, I was brought back to dayside as a rewrite man, another forgotten role in journalism. Reporters on the street would call the office, get a rewrite person on the phone, recite all the pertinent facts of the story they were working on, and the rewrite desk would compose the story. It was good training in making sense of disparate facts and in writing quickly. Once, working rewrite on the evening shift, I had no sooner typed the first version of a breaking story then editor Klatt ripped the page out of my typewriter, rushed back to his desk, and immediately began to scratch through it with his pen. I suppose my career-long freedom from the curse of writer's block stems from that early newsroom experience. I learned the invaluable lesson that first drafts are not sacred, and that the writer need not belabor them. Whatever the story may be, get it down on paper (or, now, on the screen) and then make it better.

During those City News years I found my own ways of working. After getting lost on the way to assignments I made maps and street guides a permanent part of my equipment. Today (that is, in the 2020s) I rely on a GPS app that I plug into my car's Apple Play for display on the screen. But whatever stage the technology was in, knowing where I was going before setting out became a permanent part of my job. So, too, was being prepared to communicate with the "desk," that is, the editors in the office. At City News, we went to work each day with a pocketful of dimes and quarters to call in our stories from a pay phone in a bar. Today the same thing means carrying a charging cord in case the battery on my smartphone runs low. But at every stage a reporter must carry the tools of the trade.

And at City News I took the first steps toward becoming a fast writer. Writing stories quickly isn't the definition of good journalism or of good writing in general. But getting to a final draft quickly is a useful skill in any writing situation, and perhaps most of all in newsrooms. Delivering your publishable copy on time, or even early, accomplishes many things: it keeps your editors happy, allows more time for other work, and—no small point here—it gets a journalist home for dinner instead of for the eleven o'clock news.

Long after I left City News, during my long career at the *Detroit Free Press*, I got a reputation as a fast writer, even spooky fast. I've been known to turn out a thoughtful fifty-inch column in an hour or two, which is about as fast as you can get words onto a page. Some of that speed of composition has come from writing stories for so many years that I can almost, as Frank Lloyd Wright once said of his buildings, just shake a new one out of my sleeve. And I've trained myself to try to compose at the speed of thought, as if telling myself a story and taking it down as the thoughts occur to me. (And thank you to Fr. Joseph Dunn in sophomore year of high school, who taught us touch typing, possibly the single most practical course of my entire education.)

But writing fast is more than experience, and it's not a rare gift. It's a skill, and it can be learned.

I trace my ability to compose quickly back to my City News days. After I had graduated from the midnight police beat and rewrite desk to the day shift, my editors sent me to the Cook County Criminal Courts building at Twenty-sixth and California, a hulking limestone pile with enormous high-ceilinged courtrooms at which judges presided like gods. One of my jobs as the City News beat reporter was to check daily for new indictments from the grand jury. Any major indictment would merit a press conference by the county's top attorney, but the more routine stuff simply got filed in the clerk's office. And each day I would stop by, say hello to the women behind the counter, and sift through the pile for anything worth a few lines.

My first day doing that, I selected three I thought worth something, took good notes, and dropped a dime into the hall pay phone to get the City News rewrite desk. My police reporting up to then had been done the old-school way, me calling in a bunch of facts to a rewrite person who then composed the actual story. But this first morning at the courthouse, my colleague on rewrite told me the courts reporters just dictated their stories, that is, composed them on the fly. I had never dictated a story in my life and told her so, but she encouraged me to try. I fumbled through the first one—"A Cook County grand jury indicted. . . ." I found the second one easier, and by the third I was rattling it off. The trick was to see the three- or four-paragraph story as a series of boxes that had to be filled in with name, age, the charges, the possible sentence, the name of the judge who caught the case, and so on. A typical example (I've made this one up) might go like this:

> A Cook County grand jury on Monday indicted an Oak Park bank officer for stealing funds from his bank.
>
> The indictment alleges that Thomas Murphy, 56, of Oak Park stole as much as $1 million from the Oak Park Dime Savings & Loan between 1972 and 1974.
>
> He faces six counts of theft, bank fraud, and embezzlement. The charges carry a maximum sentence of 10 years in prison.
>
> The case was assigned to Cook County Circuit Judge William Smith.

All pretty basic. And all pretty easy once you got the hang of it. Countless basic wire service stories have been written that way. Except that seeing stories as a series of boxes to be filled in stayed with me, even as I graduated to much longer and more complicated stories. Thinking of the empty boxes to be filled helped me see the holes in my information and helped me organize my stories once I had the reporting done.

Transcribing a tape-recorded interview is the least favorite part of a reporter's chores. A one-hour interview may take four hours to transcribe, and the process can be tedious as you inch a tape forward to get each word right. There are now (in the 2020s) online transcription services that one might use, but those didn't exist when I was starting out and even today many cost-cutting newspapers cannot afford that luxury. But I gradually learned to shorten the time needed to get what I wanted from a tape. (Before I get to it, let me emphasize that I believe thoroughly in taping my interviews. I'm especially keen in my writing to use the longer quotes, often two or three sentences together, that capture the flavor and nuance of a conversation. It's impossible to get that right without a tape recording; no one's memory or "ear" is good enough to capture long quotes verbatim, and I loathe the notion that one can "fill in" missing words in a quote by guessing. Over the years my tape recorders have evolved from the clunky foot-long models to slim pocket-sized sets and then to an app on my iPhone today.)

I learned to never transcribe an entire interview unless I was publishing it as a question-and-answer piece. Instead I fast forward through the tape to find the quotes I want and just transcribe those—a process that takes minutes not hours. And I developed my own little device to find those quotes on the tape. Whenever someone said something notable during an interview, I would glance at my recorder, note the time of the quote in my notepad, and add a couple of little quote marks, something like:

9:30 " "

This would tell me later that nine minutes and thirty seconds into the tape I'd find a quote that I might want to use. I'd come back from my interviews with my notebook filled with little notations like that, sometimes with a word or two attached to remind me what the quote was about. And I would go straight to those points in the recording and transcribe what I needed. I saw that this method cut my transcribing time dramatically. Back at my desk, I could pull out three or four quotable bits in a matter of minutes. It helped enormously on deadline and it gave me the ability to use those longer quotations that added depth and nuance to a piece.

If any of these techniques that I found useful can help another journalist, then good. But these are not the essence of the job. Like Balzac's fifty cups of coffee a day or Hemingway's little blue composition books in Paris, each writer needs to come up with ways to get the words on the page, whatever works for her or him. But the essence of the job is the commitment. Once committed to the trade, the rest is details. I had already made the commitment that first January day when I started work. And the commitment of that twenty-four-year-old remains still in the work I do in my seventies.

* * *

Nelson Rockefeller may be the only person to serve as vice president of the United States who's better known for roles other than that. He's better remembered today as heir to the Rockefeller industrial fortune, as an art collector, as three-term governor of New York state, and as a three-time failed presidential hopeful. But it was as vice president under Gerald Ford in the mid-'70s that Rockefeller visited the Chicago area while I was reporting for the City News Bureau.

The visit was a thank-you call on Republican supporters along the north shore and was meant to solidify support for Ford's reelection bid. I covered the various press events where reporters tried in multiple ways to get Rockefeller to say he wanted to run for president again and where Rockefeller in multiple ways denied it. The banquet that evening was the usual dull political affair: lots of forced jollity from a lot of people who probably wished to be somewhere else. But at one break in the action, with nobody at the microphones for a while, I left the press pen and walked up to chat with Rockefeller for a few moments. A reporter could still do that in those days long before 9/11 made everyone so security conscious. I don't remember much of what we said; I recall telling him of my family's New York roots and he responded with a compliment on the Chicago area. Like I said, nothing much transpired. But it was one of those occasions that illustrate one of the chief perks of a journalist's life: you get to see, listen to, and meet interesting people *all the time*.

A few other examples: In the fall of 1975 Egyptian President Anwar Sadat came to Chicago as part of his state visit to America. The City News Bureau, like all the media outlets, had reporters staffing his appearances. My assignment that night was twofold: first to interview the protesters across Michigan Avenue from the Hilton where Sadat would speak; these were in two groups, pro-Israel demonstrators protesting what they saw as Sadat's failure to live in peace with Israelis, and fundamentalist Muslims who condemned Sadat as too secular. After calling in my notes to the rewrite desk I took up my post for the second part of my assignment, to stand with other reporters by the entrance to watch his arrival in case anything untoward happened. Sadat's limo pulled up and he and Chicago Mayor Richard J. Daley emerged and walked slowly to the entrance of the hotel. Sadat nodded and smiled to us, preternaturally calm, I thought, for a man riding atop one of the world's tigers and reviled by so many.

And I remember thinking that there's an odd couple you don't see together every day, the legendary Boss Daley of Chicago and the beleaguered president of Egypt, side by side on the red carpet. Odd, indeed, but in journalism that sort of thing happens.

Another day the famed Nazi hunter Simon Wiesenthal came to Chicago. The moral authority emanating from the man was palpable. As he spoke of his personal journey, as a rare surviving Jew from his hometown, where thousands of Jews were slaughtered in the Holocaust, and of dedicating his life to the pursuit of the murderers, I felt I was in the presence of a man of history.

* * *

We were young, of course, all in our early to midtwenties, with all the quirks and enthusiasms of youth. Along with my besties (Greg Small, later with AP's Honolulu bureau, Bob Rowley, much later spokesman for Northwestern University, and many other friends) we'd meet after work at Billy Goat's or Miller's Pub, where we'd bitch about our bosses and drink too much beer. If you had asked us who we wanted to be, I suppose most or all of us would have cited Mike Royko. Back in the mid-1970s, I knew Mike Royko the way any Chicagoan did, as an avid reader of his columns in the *Daily News* and, later on, in the *Sun-Times* and *Tribune*. But my interest went beyond a Chicagoan's daily shot of Royko's acerbic wit. Just beginning my own journalism career, my hope, like any of us "City News kids," was to move on to a major newspaper, and Mike Royko was everything we aspired to be—the smartest and savviest don't-give-a-damn journalist in town.

Royko was a workingman's columnist, poking fun at faddists and charlatans and do-gooders and all the newfangled computers that always seemed to spit out nonsense. Most of all he targeted politicians, from Mayor Richard J. Daley ("The Great Dumpling") and his toady aldermen in City Council to the whole venal crowd of fixers and hangers-on whose motto, Royko suggested, should be the Latin "Ubi Est Mea"—"Where's mine?" That Royko produced the funniest, most readable column in town was high achievement; that he did it *daily*, for decades, when most columnists wrote two or perhaps three times a week, marked journalistic success on a level beyond mere mortals. Naturally he had a Pulitzer in his pocket. In his later years, Royko's streetwise average-Joe take on certain issues of the day, like the women's movement and gay rights, led critics to label him a dinosaur. In the 1990s, David Remnick in the *New Yorker* dismissed Royko's later columns as "hollow carping." But in the mid-'70s, to a cub reporter like me, Royko was everything I aspired to be.

For the most part, all my hero worship was done from a distance. I hadn't met Royko yet. For a novice reporter like I was at the time—young, callow, my ambition offset by my inexperience—Royko was as near as his daily column but still remote—someone we didn't see up close and personal in our young lives.

But sometimes we did. Royko famously loved his softball games, the White Sox, a beer at Billy Goat's tavern on Lower Wacker Drive beneath his newspaper building. It would be hard to be a young City News kid in Chicago then, going everywhere and talking with everyone, imbibing the flavor of journalism with the beer and *cheezborgers* at Billy Goat's, to not glimpse Royko at least occasionally.

I had three such encounters. I doubt any of them left an impression on Royko himself once I was out of sight. But for an eager City News kid in the '70s, they meant a lot. And now as the years pass and only those Chicagoans middle-aged or older can recall the excitement of reading Royko each day, I cherish my few moments with him even more.

My first occasion, other than seeing Royko at the bar in Billy Goat's, was when he interviewed a bunch of us to be his leg man, a researcher that helped him with his column. I applied, got an interview, and walked (or more likely floated on air) over to the *Daily News* building off Michigan Avenue for my meeting with the great man. I was one of twenty or so young applicants for the job. Royko gave me perhaps fifteen minutes. He was everything I pictured—sleeves rolled up, tie askew—while I was everything a job candidate shouldn't be—over-eager, awed by the man I was meeting. I doubt I made much of an impression. At one point Royko asked me what foreign languages I spoke, and it was so clearly a throwaway question that I knew even then the job would never be mine. At least I learned a little about keeping my spirits under control when interviewing for a job.

It wasn't long after that that I had my second encounter. I had finished my shift at City News late one evening, around midnight, and went to Billy Goat's for a beer, awaiting the arrival of my friend and coworker Neil. I had the place to myself but for Mike Royko and one of his softball buddies at the far end of the bar. Royko's love of softball was well known in town, and this late evening he and his teammate were dressed in their blue softball uniforms and obviously drinking postgame. After I'd been waiting a few minutes, Neil walked down the steps into Billy Goat's and, before he could come over to me, Royko hopped off his stool and demanded to know Neil's name. Then Royko turned to Warren, the stolid bartender, and yelled at the top of his voice, "Warren! Get Neil a fucking drink!" He repeated this command twice more, each time top of voice. Then he turned to Neil and said, "There! I just gave you a lesson in assertiveness," assertiveness being one of the catchwords of the day. And with that he invited Neil to sit with them.

So I headed over to join them. I tried to hold my giddiness in check, probably only half successfully. To have met the great man at all was cool enough for an ambitious young Chicago reporter; to have a drink with him in the hallowed Billy Goat's was the topper. And while he had shown he could be loud and boisterous, I don't mean to give the impression he was drunk; comfortably loose, perhaps; but even then I sense it was a calculated looseness. Royko was so famous then that being out in public demanded a kind of performance from him. He could no longer be just the scribbler who played softball with friends; surrounded by the public, he had to be a larger-than-life figure.

Take what happened perhaps an hour later. Leaving Billy Goat's, we all piled into one of their cars (mine was left parked where it would get towed come morning if I wasn't careful), and we headed to not one, not two, but I think three bars throughout the rest of the night. At the first, Royko as ever drew a crowd. I remember one young tough looked like he wanted to pick a fight, although nothing untoward happened. At one point Royko took me up to a young woman at the bar and, draping his arm around my shoulder, regaled her with high praise for what a great guy I was and why she should definitely get to know me. Then, after a minute or so of that blather, he turned to me and said, "Now, what's your name?" It was Royko as performance artist.

It was perhaps five a.m. when Neil and I finally called it quits. Royko was having pizza with another young woman in an after-hours place, and it was clear our night had run its course. I got back to my car as the sky was pearling with early morn. Luckily, no ticket, and I hadn't gotten towed.

We knew we were lucky to have him in Chicago, and at no time did we realize that more than in 1975 when Ben Bradlee of the *Washington Post* tried to lure Royko to DC to work for him. These were the post-Watergate years, when Bradlee and his Woodward-and-Bernstein team were celebrated throughout the journalism world. Little wonder he would try to hire the best and most celebrated columnist in the nation. Royko spent a few days down in DC, talking to Bradlee and his team at the *Post*, and since his visit had become widely talked about in our journalism orbit, we Chicagoans held our collective breath hoping Royko would tell the *Post* no and remain in the Windy City. That, in fact, is what happened, and Royko continued to write his columns in Chicago until his death more than twenty years later.

Years later I asked Bradlee about his attempt to lure Royko to the *Post*. The idea, Bradlee told me, was to have Royko do for the United States Congress what he had done for Chicago aldermen: pin them to the wall, expose their foibles, mock them as needed. When I asked him why he thought Royko had opted to stay in Chicago, Bradlee suggested that coming to DC may have looked too great a reach for a Chicago boy—maybe he was intimidated by the scope of the Capital scene.

But I prefer another explanation, and it comes straight from the horse's mouth. At the end of the week he had spent down in Washington visiting the *Post*, I was getting some dinner at (where else?) Billy Goat's, and Royko walked in and took a seat at the bar near a friend. I was seated a few feet away. The friend asked the very question all of Chicago was asking then: "So, Mike, how'd it go?" Royko's answer spoke volumes about how gritty Chicago matched up against highbrow Washington. "They're nice people," he said. "But Jesus! So serious!"

*   *   *

And so in this way I progressed through four years at City News, graduating from cops and the rewrite desk to cover city hall, Cook County affairs, state agencies, the Chicago Board of Education during the bitter battles over school desegregation. The goal of any CNB kid was to move on to one of the Chicago dailies; that had been the career path for the past century. But by my time that pipeline was closing. Since Watergate and the appeal of the book and movie *All the President's Men*, the newspaper industry was flooding with young people hoping to emulate Woodward and Bernstein (I for one grew my hair long like Dustin Hoffman playing Bernstein), and the Chicago papers no longer automatically called up City News staffers with regularity. Instead we were forced to look far afield for our next jobs. After much effort and an unrecorded number of résumés mailed, I got an offer from the Rochester, New York, *Democrat & Chronicle*.

I had mixed feelings about leaving Chicago. It may be America's best news town, and I would have been glad to spend the rest of my career there. But as with transferring around the country for my father's job with GM, I probably took more from my subsequent career moves than I gave up. At any rate, in my late twenties by then and unmarried (the all-consuming City News life was hardly ideal for attracting a girlfriend), I was ready to give something new a try.

Among the farewells from my friends and coworkers, one colleague, John Wolfe, offered a sort of benediction. "Your salad days are over, kid," he told me. "You're a vet."

4

Upstate New York

By the late 1970s, when I left Chicago for Upstate New York, the twin crises facing American newspapers and American cities were both accelerating. It says a lot about how we dodge our troubles that neither newspapers nor cities were awake to the dangers facing them.

First, newspapers. It's no secret that all cities once enjoyed many more daily and weekly newspapers than were operating in the 1970s. Many of the older ones had closed or been gobbled up by stronger competitors. When I joined City News in 1974, there were four main Chicago dailies—the morning *Tribune* and *Sun-Times* and the afternoon *Daily News* and *Chicago Today*. But America was losing its afternoon newspapers—once the daily reading of factory hands getting off shift—as changing lifestyles made those afternoon papers obsolete. The *Daily News* and *Chicago Today* both folded, as did numbers of p.m. papers across the nation. But the great morning dailies only felt more empowered than ever by their weaker counterparts' demise. No one saw what was coming.

And American cities, especially those in the heartland, were likewise ignoring the danger signs. In the postwar years the desire to leave behind the crowded cities for a life in the suburbs was already bleeding away jobs and residents to the newer communities in the meadows and cornfields. My new home of Rochester had seen its population peak at over three hundred thousand in the 1950s; when I arrived in the late 1970s, it had fallen to about 250,000 and would fall to almost two hundred thousand in the twenty-first century. Almost all cities were losing residents and jobs to the suburbs. Detroit, where I spent the majority of my career, peaked at nearly two million residents in the 1950 Census; by the time I semi-retired in Detroit in late 2019, only about 640,000 remained. Buffalo, St. Louis, and countless smaller towns like Flint and Youngstown and Allentown were all losing people to the new suburbs beyond their borders.

Yet the early responses were ineffectual or, worse, drove more residents to the exits. Cities raised taxes on remaining residents, rammed expressways through still viable neighborhoods, and did little to stem racist real estate practices that helped create the sharp racial divide for which America's cities had become known.

In years to come, I would focus on this worsening crisis of cities far and wide, from former steel towns like Youngstown, Ohio, to one-time manufacturing hubs in Europe like Leipzig, Germany, which lost 90 percent of its manufacturing jobs when the Soviet Union collapsed, depriving Leipzig of the cash that had propped up its factories. All different cities, yet in many ways all the same, struggling to reinvent themselves in a harsh new economic and political environment. German scholars came up with the phrase "shrinking cities" to capture the phenomenon and calculated that some three hundred cities around the world with populations greater than one hundred thousand had been significantly reduced from their peak years.

My new home of Rochester would be hard hit by the turn of the economic wheel. When I arrived its main employer, Eastman Kodak, still lorded it as the "Great Yellow Father" (so called for the yellow film boxes it sold by the millions) and employed some sixty thousand workers at its Kodak Park in town. But the company missed the technological turn when it ignored until too late the arrival of digital cameras that made film all but obsolete. Today, well into the 2020s, the company employs no more than a few thousand workers in Rochester.

*　*　*

My understanding of this nationwide, even worldwide, urban crisis would grow with time, and so would my ability to write about it. But that was to come. I admit I was focused mostly on my own troubles when I moved in my late twenties to Rochester, New York, in 1978.

I had been hired by the *Democrat & Chronicle* to work as a bureau chief covering some of Rochester's outlying areas, but when I got there they asked me to spend a few weeks instead on the night copy desk, for as city editor Tim Bunn told me, "We're desperate for good copy editors." A few weeks turned into two years, despite my extreme distaste at being desk-bound while all the reporters were out chasing stories and getting bylines, and my growing resentment that I'd been treated to a bait-and-switch job offer. I complained enough that I finally got moved to a reporting job. But by then there were other troubles roiling the Rochester newsroom.

Once upon a time, newspapers enjoyed local ownership by wealthy families in each city. These families operated their papers not just to make money, which they did in spectacular fashion, but as a public trust. The owners were kingmakers and boosters, and their reign seemed unlikely ever to end.

But in time these paternalistic families did lose control, for much the same reasons that affect any family-owned companies a generation or two or three down the line. In some cases the later generations of trust-account kids want the family to cash out; at other times sibling rivalry can rip apart a once-stable arrangement. In 1987, Alex S. Jones of the *New York Times* won a Pulitzer for "The Fall of the House of Bingham," a saga of how the family that owned the Louisville *Courier Journal* had split apart over the newspaper's fate. When, in city after city, these longtime owners sold, rising newspaper corporations stood ready to snatch the prizes.

These growing media companies were a mixed lot. Knight Newspapers was founded by John S. Knight when he inherited the *Akron Beacon Journal* from his father, Charles Knight, in 1933. The company merged in 1974 with Ridder Publications, and for another generation Knight-Ridder was among the classiest of the media giants, publishing thirty-two newspapers including the *Miami Herald*, the *Philadelphia Inquirer*, and the *Detroit Free Press*, and regularly winning Pulitzers (including several at its Detroit paper). Another and different sort of company, Gannett Corporation, founded in 1923 by Frank Gannett in Rochester, New York, grew out of a gaggle of papers in that state to become the biggest newspaper company in the nation. Under CEO Al Neuharth, the company earned a reputation for prioritizing profits; Neuharth famously quipped, when asked how to pronounce Gannett, that the emphasis was on the net. Among many other papers, it owned the conservative *Detroit News*, a contrast to Knight-Ridder's more progressive *Detroit Free Press*.

Gannett's flagship newspaper was still the Rochester *Democrat & Chronicle* when I arrived there in 1978. If the City News Bureau had run chaotically at times, throwing young journalists in their early twenties into the maelstrom of Chicago politics and crime, my new Gannett employer was straitlaced and hierarchical. Perhaps this mirrored the culture of Rochester itself (not for nothing did writer G. Curtis Gerling entitle his 1957 book about the city *Smugtown, USA*). But the atmosphere in our newsroom owed even more to the looming corporate presence of Gannett. The corporation already had a reputation of imposing top-down directives on its many newspapers, and that reputation of heavy, even oppressive corporate control only grew with time. Some of us in the newsroom took to calling the company the Evil Empire and its true believers as Gannettoids. No surprise that during my four years at the paper I grew increasingly estranged from my employer.

The personifications of my unhappiness were two top editors. Bob Giles was editor at the morning *Democrat & Chronicle* and afternoon *Times-Union*; his top deputy, Nancy Woodhull, was an editor at the *Times-Union* before becoming our boss at the *Democrat & Chronicle*. Both Giles and Woodhull became famous in the newspaper industry. Giles went on to run the Gannett-owned *Detroit News* (we'll meet him again in a later chapter), wrote a well-received book on newsroom management, and capped his career by serving as director of the prestigious Nieman fellowship for journalists at Harvard University. Woodhull, too, went on to bigger things, becoming the first managing editor of Gannett's newly launched *USA Today* in 1982 and a top news executive for Gannett. She became an icon for women and diversity in the newspaper industry before she died of cancer in 1997 at the age of fifty-two.

Despite their credits, from the vantage point of someone working in the Rochester newsroom around 1980, these two icons and their aides were difficult. Gannett's management style is nothing if not heavy, and Giles and Woodhull and their aides embodied that style in Rochester. There was a pervasive feeling among us rankers that favorites were being played and that corporate directives were eroding the freedom traditionally enjoyed by reporters, photographers, and lower-ranking editors. It seemed that corporate control of almost every aspect of our work was becoming the norm. It showed up in ways large and small. Once a department head told his staff in a memo that sick days weren't permitted on Mondays or Fridays because (he implied) a staffer calling in sick then obviously just wanted a longer weekend; we called it the "clean death" memo (as in don't make a mess when you keel over at your desk). It was so ridiculous that it was quickly rescinded. But it wasn't so easy to parry other directives.

Editors always have the final say on how a story reads; that's their job. But now editors were rewriting openings of stories wholesale (the first paragraph or "lede") as if reporters were no more than note takers. It rankled us to have our role diminished this way. Once an editor came to me as I was about to write my story and gushed that they were going to give me free rein on how I wrote it, that I could really have some fun with it. Then he added, "Now, here's your lede."

Jack Welch, the famed CEO of General Electric, later became the apostle for a ruthless management style that promoted the top tier of performers, berated the middle tier to do better, and sacked the bottom ranks. Before Welch ever took over at GE, Gannett was doing something like that in Rochester and at its other newspapers. Criticism of the newsroom staff by top editors became frequent and at times nasty. In the hands of Gannett managers the annual review became a tool to deny raises to supposedly poor performers. I suffered my share of demeaning dressing-downs. I'm generally thought to be a good journalist. But I got more negative reviews and took more criticism in my handful of years in Rochester than in all the other forty-odd years of my career combined.

Eventually I saw it wasn't going to get any better for me and I moved an hour east on the New York State Thruway to the *Post-Standard* in Syracuse, a much happier experience for me in every way. It, too, was corporately owned, by the Newhouse family, but the owners had a lighter hand there. Editors at the *Post-Standard* respected reporters, worked with them to improve stories without stomping on egos, and generally ran a more benign workplace. My outlook improved. I felt I was back on track.

Years later, long after I'd moved in 1987 to the *Detroit Free Press*, a Knight-Ridder newspaper, the unthinkable happened. In 2005 Knight-Ridder sold the *Free Press* to Gannett. Once more I was in the hands of the company that had made my life miserable a quarter-century earlier. This time, though, the freewheeling culture of the *Free Press* newsroom was able to ward off the evil spirits for a time. And by then I was well enough established in my field to have some protection from arbitrary directives. But there was no escaping Gannett; the corporate side of the business slowly but relentlessly eroded the local identity of its many papers including Detroit's, sweeping us all under the heading of the *USA Today* network. This octopus at one point arbitrarily swapped out the Old English font of the *Detroit Free Press* logo on our website—a much-loved image in use for a century or more—for one of Gannett's standard block-letter logos. We bitched and howled enough that the company gave us our logo back. But, as I say, most corporate moves were not so easily parried.

With Knight-Ridder going out of existence and newspapers failing everywhere as Google and Facebook took away our advertising base, I could console myself during the latter years of my career with a mordant thought: Gannett or not, at least we were still in business. My paycheck still cleared. But that consolation sufficed only for a time.

* * *

I don't know if the ten thousand–hour rule has any scientific validity—the idea that one needs to practice a craft for that number of hours to master it. But I do know it took awhile for my career in journalism to feel fully on track, especially after the unhappy stint in Rochester had shaken my confidence.

That first week in Syracuse (this was in June 1982, and I was in my early thirties), my new editor at the *Post-Standard* asked me to do a story he'd been pitching to his staff for weeks with no takers. An older neighborhood known as the Hawley Avenue–Green Street Preservation District was undergoing a rapid revival, the sort of upgrading that we now call gentrification. In 1982, when I got to Syracuse, it was still mostly an inner urban neighborhood with a lot of older homes, including some stately houses from the nineteenth century and others smaller and more modest, and the district was just beginning to see new owners buying and renovating the better homes. But a rash of fires there lately had damaged some of the older houses; the cause of the fires was a mix of malicious mischief and perhaps spite arson. My editor wanted someone to write about the contrasts in a neighborhood undergoing revival and setbacks at the same time.

That same day I spent the afternoon walking the neighborhood, stepping up to the front porches and knocking on doors, talking with neighbors, both old-timers and newcomers, and then called the fire chief to ask about the fires. My story opened:

> There's a battle going on in the Green Street neighborhood between the builders and the burners.
>
> In Jean Piquet's case, the burners have won.

The story quoted the people I had interviewed, including Ms. Piquet, a late-middle-aged woman whose home had been damaged by arson next door. Her story contrasted with those of developers who were too busy profiting to worry about the fires. At the end of the piece I returned to Piquet:

> But for Jean Piquet of Green Street, the latest fires have been enough. She's staying in a hotel because her building has no electricity, and she hopes to move soon to the north side.
>
> She says she began suffering heart problems more than a year ago because of the frequent fires. When the first of three arsons next door occurred June 6, she suffered a heart attack that kept her hospitalized for 10 days, she says.
>
> She is asked how many fires there have been. She counts five within a block of her home.
>
> "The one around the corner, six, and the one up the hill, seven," she says.
>
> "It got the best of me," she confesses. "It's just been too many."

My editor was delighted. He told everyone he had tried for weeks to interest his reporters in the story until the new guy showed up and did it in a day.

After my years of disappointment at the Rochester paper, this had gone so easily for me that I experienced a new feeling. It was a realization that, *yes, I can do this job*. Eight years from the day I took my first tentative steps toward being a police reporter for the City News Bureau of Chicago, I finally felt like I could report and write any story. It was a good feeling, and it stayed with me. The confidence I gained did as much as anything to carry me through all the years of journalism that followed.

* * *

I enjoyed my four years in Syracuse, both writing for the paper and taking up hiking and skiing in the lovely setting of the Finger Lakes region and around Lake Placid in the Adirondacks. After the stresses and misgivings in Rochester, I thoroughly enjoyed my colleagues at the *Post-Standard*, and together we broke many stories and published many investigative pieces that sometimes rattled local city and business leaders. In one, I reported on how the mergers and acquisitions craze then roiling corporate America was impacting local communities like Syracuse. Two of the town's major firms, Carrier Air Conditioning and the lesser-known Crouse-Hinds, a specialty lighting company, had been gobbled up by bigger corporate buyers recently. And naturally we wanted to know what happens when top corporate headquarters, for decades suppliers of both jobs and tax base and charitable support, disappear in a wave of mergers. My three-part series, headlined "Taking Over: What Mergers Have Meant to Syracuse," opened June 11, 1984, with a look at the turmoil at Crouse-Hinds after the takeover by an outside buyer:

> There is an office on the first floor of the Crouse-Hinds building at Wolf and Seventh North streets that some workers call "Death Valley."
>
> Chris Whiting, the former chairman of the board, built the office for himself as a cozy retirement hideaway. But for the

last three years it has served another purpose. Executives fallen from favor and with little to do spend their final weeks and months in the office before leaving the firm for good.

"Don't move down there," goes a warning around the company, "because your next move's out the door."

Then there was my assessment of the results, or rather lack of results, of an economic development campaign by the local Chamber known as Greater Syracuse. It was designed to lure new employers and new industries, but the results were dismal. Under the heading "Will Syracuse Get Its Share?" my opening ran:

> A cynic might liken the Greater Syracuse campaign to John Connally's presidential bid in 1980. Big John spent $10 million during the primaries and won exactly one delegate.
>
> In the two years since its announcement, the Greater Syracuse program has spent about three-quarters of a million dollars to lure new businesses to Syracuse. In return, the campaign has achieved about as much in the way of hard results as Connally did.

And in a third project, I wrote the inside tale of another corporate takeover, this one of a local airline called Empire that was acquired by the larger Piedmont Aviation (itself, of course, long since absorbed into today's handful of giant airlines). Titled "The Fall of an Empire," the opening segment ran:

> It was late afternoon, Saturday Sept. 28. Carrying his passport, Paul Quackenbush boarded Empire Airlines Flight 85 in Utica and flew to Kennedy Airport in New York. Quackenbush, the founder, chairman and president of Empire, changed there to a Pam Am overseas flight to France.
>
> Quackenbush was embarking on a secret mission, a rescue attempt to save his company from being purchased by North Carolina–based Piedmont Aviation. In Nice, France, a fashionable city on the Riviera, he hoped to meet with representatives of Pam Am who were holding a high-level conference.

Quackenbush hoped to arrange a deal with Pam Am that would allow Empire to retain a measure of its independence and save it from disappearing into the Piedmont fold.

But it was not to be. When Quackenbush flew home Sunday, Sept. 29, on a British Airways Concorde, he did not carry with him sufficient promises to ward off Piedmont. And within days, the deal with Piedmont was sealed.

The subjects of these stories generally hated them. After the Crouse-Hinds piece ran, some of their execs came to our newsroom to complain. When I introduced my editors to them and mentioned my own name, the head p.r. woman said with a sneer, "We know who *you* are."

But corporate mergers and their impact on local communities was an important and growing story. America has fostered a winner-take-all economy for a long time, and it's the smaller communities in the heartland that often pay the price for the success of the biggest firms and biggest metros. It's the job of newspapers to tell that story in all the detail it can, even if our stories are no more than the proverbial still small voice of conscience. The catastrophic decline of newspapers in America is also a result of these forces, and ironically, the more it is needed the less this basic watchdog journalism can be done.

Perhaps surprisingly, the criticism that sometimes (often?) came my way from corporate leaders didn't trouble me much. I had the support of my colleagues at the newspaper, and many readers let us know they appreciated the coverage we were giving them. One local businessman who liked my work described my stories as "tickling the dinosaur's tail." A newspaper reporter can do that; few others in society have the freedom to do so. One of the tragedies of the decline of newspapers in our time is that fewer and fewer people enjoy that freedom to speak out without fear or favor.

There was an added benefit for me in all this. The *Post-Standard* was winning journalism awards for its range of first-rate coverage, and I took home some of those. My "Taking Over" series on mergers won an award called the Champion-Tuck, a national business writing prize awarded by the Amos Tuck School of Business at Dartmouth. It came with a $5,000 prize, the biggest windfall of my young career.

It was gratifying to do good work and win some awards for it. But like any reporter I had ambitions to move on to a major paper, and the way to do that, or at least one way to advance, was to win one of several major journalism fellowships at universities around the nation. These fellowships give midcareer journalists a nine-month paid sabbatical and the chance to study in classes throughout the university. They also serve as recruiting grounds for larger newspapers, magazines, and broadcast outlets. The most famous of these fellowships was and is the Neiman program at Harvard; Stanford and the University of Michigan have their own journalism fellowships, Yale offered one focusing on the law, and Columbia University operates its Bagehot Fellowship in economic journalism, named for Walter Bagehot, the nineteenth-century British editor of the *Economist* magazine.

From the beginning I thought the Bagehot program was the best for me as a business journalist, in part because I tried to model my writing after that of Chris Welles, a freelance writer famed for his intricate narratives of business failures and who also ran the Bagehot program at Columbia. But I applied for all the different fellowships almost from the time I got to Syracuse, and routinely got rejections. I kept at it, coming close with Columbia in my third year of trying when Welles called to say budget cuts had reduced his fellowship that year from ten places down to six; if he'd had full funding, he said, I would have made it. Almost ready to give up, I tried one more time in 1986, had interviews at Stanford and Michigan, and was told later I was runner-up for the Stanford fellowship. Only Columbia was yet to respond. Thinking I had struck out yet again, I was stunned when Mary Bralove, Welles's successor running the Columbia program, called me to say that my clips had gotten better year after year and that I had been selected as one of seven Bagehot Fellows for the 1986–87 year.

5

My New York Year

In a 1986 segment on *60 Minutes*, novelist James A. Michener recounted how his experiences in the South Pacific during World War II profoundly changed the trajectory of his life. Already in his midthirties by wartime, Michener had been a teacher and a textbook editor in his prewar years. But as he told interviewer Diane Sawyer when the two visited one of the islands Michener knew, the two years he spent in the Pacific for the Navy allowed him to discover his voice and gave him the germ of ideas for his Pulitzer-winning book, *Tales of the South Pacific*. Speaking metaphorically, he told Sawyer, "When I came here, I was a boy of about nineteen. When I left, I was a man of forty. And you're real lucky when you find a place that can do that for you."

Something similar if less dramatic happened to me during my year in New York. In my midthirties, I had already been a working journalist a dozen years by then, had held jobs in Chicago, Rochester, and Syracuse, written hundreds of stories, and pocketed prizes for my work. But still I was working within the limited canvas, the nearer horizon. New York changed that. The city was hardly new to me; I had been born there, visited relatives many times, took the occasional holiday there. But living, studying, and exploring the city in the coming year with a new intensity and curiosity opened new vistas, gave me and my work a maturity and direction it had lacked. There are many pivot points in our lives, some more important than others. For me, the ten months I spent in New York in 1986–87 upped my game for all the years to come.

It was a glorious time to be in New York on somebody else's money, even if my stipend from Columbia, $14,000 (or about $38,000 in inflation-adjusted 2024 dollars), required careful budgeting on my part. I had a room in a Columbia residence for graduate students and visitors at 119th and Morningside Drive, a small unit with a bedroom and sitting room and a tiny hot-plate kitchen area, with laundry machines in the basement where residents stood elbow to elbow vying for a washer and dryer. There were seven of us Bagehot Fellows, plus our director, Mary Bralove, based in a small office in the journalism school. One of our fellows, Elyse Tanouye, later won a Pulitzer with the *Wall Street Journal*. A Malaysian journalist, Yee Mee Fah, cooked us Malay dishes and loved sports; once we went to Madison Square Garden to see Kansas beat St. John's 62–60 on no-time-left free throws. I became good buddies with two of my fellow Bagehots, Pam Luecke from the *Louisville Courier Journal* and Debra Silimeo, later a leading public relations consultant in Washington, DC. When the other fellows were busy, Pam, Deb, and I, calling ourselves "The Trio," went to plays together and once to New York's nightclub of the moment, The Tunnel, named because the far end opened to an unused underground train tunnel. And we played lots of games of Trivial Pursuit when we weren't studying or taking field trips or otherwise working.

The rules of our fellowship were that we could take classes throughout the university, pass/fail permitted for most but at least one class each term for credit. The idea was to put just enough of a burden on us that we would work hard for one grade and not just skip classes to prowl the city. But once among the ambitious MBA crowd at the graduate business school where we took most of our classes, we journalists grew competitive, too, and most of us opted for full credit, requiring a lot more work and worry. It created an extra burden but helped us master the material. Having made that effort the first semester, I resolved to take it a little easier my second term to enjoy more of New York and what clearly was rare access to one of the world's great cities.

My one indulgence was going to plays, both on and off Broadway. The big show that year was August Wilson's play *Fences* with James Earl Jones. I ordered my ticket well in advance to get a good seat and was moved by Jones's performance. My favorites that year were *The Widow Claire*, one of Horton Foote's cycle of plays mainly about his father, and *Coastal Disturbances*, with two young actors about to be famous, Annette Bening and Tim Daly. I saw a couple dozen plays, indulging a love of theater that has never left me.

I found less expensive ways to entertain myself, too. The simplest thing was walking the streets of New York. Leaving my apartment at 119th and Morningside, I would step over to the subway stop at 116th, catch a train down to, say, Times Square, and take my time strolling back the sixty blocks or so, meandering through Central Park or window shopping or grabbing a pizza slice somewhere. Then as now, I found that even a single block in New York often showed more life, more interesting architecture, more variety, and more vitality than entire cities do elsewhere. I still remember one morning when I took the subway down to a Barnes & Noble bookstore in lower Manhattan, and as I walked along the sunlit streets, I felt surprised by a burst of pure joy just being alive in such a great city. New York will sometimes do that for you.

Besides our classes, the program scheduled field trips for us and weekly dinners with top economists and business leaders. The main event in our year was dinner with Paul Volcker, the chairman of the Federal Reserve, already a legend, indeed a demigod, for his crushing of inflation, even if it came at the cost of a brutal recession in the industrial heartland. Normally I took an active part in all of our dinner conversations, but I had a heavy cold that evening, felt miserable throughout the dinner, and maybe for that reason I didn't warm to the great man. I found him to be inscrutable, dough-faced, and impassive. In contrast to our normal seating arrangement, when the guest sat in the middle of the table with Bagehots to either side and across from him, Volcker sat at the head of the table dispensing Delphic bits of wisdom, and since we had a couple of extras that evening, the dean of Columbia's MBA program and a *Times* editor, it was less intimate and informal than we were used to. We did get Volcker going a few times; he took shots at Sears for trying to get into banking, and grumbled a little about the Wall Street merger guys putting together deals based solely on their fees. But I didn't think we got much that was new from him, and on the whole I was glad to get back to my apartment and bed.

*   *   *

There are many fine books on the craft of writing, and I've read and learned a lot from them: classics like William Zinsser's *On Writing Well*, Strunk and White's *Elements of Style*, and many more. For a young journalist eager to improve a prose style, those are good places to start. To that vast library of advice I'd like to contribute one writing tip of my own.

During my New York year as a Bagehot, my favorite of our seminar guests was Ken Auletta, the *New Yorker* writer whose 1985 saga in the *New York Times Magazine*, "Power, Greed and Glory on Wall Street: The Fall of the Lehman Brothers," had been among the best long-form business stories in many years. The story of how the Lehman Brothers investment house had fallen apart presented scenes of dramatic confrontations among the senior partners and dialogue that everyone involved had agreed was accurate. Seated at our seminar table, Auletta talked engagingly about that story and how he'd done it. But the anecdote that really stayed with me, and the one that changed the way I write my own stories, concerned one of his first encounters with the *New Yorker*'s legendary editor William Shawn.

In 1979 Auletta wrote a profile of New York City Mayor Ed Koch for the *New Yorker*. For his opening, he wanted to capture Koch's outsized ego. Koch's self-absorption could be vast; it reminded Auletta of that old Hollywood joke: *That's enough about me. Let's talk about you. What do you think of me?* So he crafted a lead that went like this:

> Friends and associates of Mayor Edward I. Koch have noticed that when the Mayor's attention wanders during discussions of the city's fiscal crisis or some other eye-glazing topic a sure way to lure him back is to change the subject to the Mayor. The truth is that the Mayor finds himself fascinating.

When the first page proofs came back from Shawn, Auletta saw that the editor changed just one word. He had crossed out the word "lure" and changed it to "bring":

> Friends and associates of Mayor Edward I. Koch have noticed that when the Mayor's attention wanders during discussions

of the city's fiscal crisis or some other eye-glazing topic a sure
way to bring him back is to change the subject to the Mayor.
The truth is that the Mayor finds himself fascinating.

That was odd, Auletta thought. The word "lure" was more evocative than the pedestrian word "bring." So he changed it back and
sent in the proofs. Sure enough, the second proofs came back from
Shawn with "lure" crossed out and "bring" once more in there. So
when Auletta met with Shawn in person for the final edit, he made
his pitch for "lure."

As Auletta told us, Shawn said, "You're right, Mr. Auletta. Lure is
a much more evocative word than bring. It is so good that it *steps on
your punchline.*" The goal, Shawn explained, was to propel the reader
to the payoff. A reader may stumble or hesitate just a moment over
"lure" since it evokes all sorts of exotic meanings. A humbler word
like "bring" in that spot carries the reader smoothly through to the
end, always the most important part of a sentence, paragraph, or story.

"Now, *that's* good editing," Auletta told us. Indeed it is. And ever
since I have tried to pay closer attention to word choice in my own
stories. It means going through my copy to change passive voice to
active voice. It means paying attention to the *last* word or phrase of
each sentence or paragraph to achieve that little *pop!* to complete the
thought and propel the reader onward. It means pruning the waste
and not just dumping a word salad on the page and calling it done.

Daily journalism is generally not thought to rank among the best
writing; it is too rushed, too confined by the space limitations of
the news "hole," too often meddled with by too many editors. But
even daily journalism can deliver a large measure of satisfaction from
careful attention to craft and style in the writing. It only requires the
writer care enough to nudge each sentence or paragraph from merely
adequate to better and on to good.

*   *   *

The most useful class at Columbia for me as a journalist interested
in understanding how the world and the economy really work was
an introduction to tax law, taught by a leading New York practitioner

named Richard "Dick" Cummins. Besides his adjunct role at Columbia he served as national director of personal financial services for Coopers & Lybrand and was special adviser to the board of directors of the New York Mets. Our class started at eight a.m. so he could get to his practice afterward. He would stand on this little platform at the head of the class and with his booming voice call on students to explain this or that famous case. One morning he called on me to explain something called the Kirby Lumber case, a decision written by Justice Oliver Wendell Holmes Jr., and when I answered, "Justice Holmes wrote it," Cummins said, "Correct. The great man himself." Then he asked me what Congress had done in response to Holmes's decision, which I fumbled, and I stalled completely when he asked me about something called Section 108 of the code. Nobody else knew either, and Cummins warned that he once had to flunk two students who didn't know the all-important Section 108. If I learned it in time for the exam, I can't for the life of me remember it today. But the best part of his class was his insider tales from his practice in the world of big-time tax law, and it's these that have stuck with me. These anecdotes exposed how the system really works in America. We got the impression Cummins was ambivalent about some of what he had to do for his clients, as he often and openly criticized the greed that he saw at work. He never knew that his stories motivated me as a journalist to focus on the hard realities of our economy; years later, covering development in Detroit, I took to calling the world of deal-making the "sleaze beat."

In one class he recounted how he had helped one of America's wealthiest families avoid a substantial tax bill. The puzzle ran like this: An elderly woman owned hundreds of thousands of shares of one of America's great corporations. She had owned her shares for so long that they had an original basis (or starting value for tax purposes) of just a penny. That stock was now worth hundreds of millions of dollars. She therefore faced a huge capital gains liability if she unloaded them. How to avoid the tax hit? Pacing back and forth on his little platform, Cummins ran through the procedure he devised. It started with the elderly wife gifting all her shares to her elderly husband, giving them outright to him. Then, anticipating that the husband would live at least another year (as required by the tax code for this to work), *he* could bequeath the shares back to his wife in his will. That triggered a 100 percent marital exemption of the inheritance tax and also created a basis stepped up to the current value of the shares, zeroing out the capital gains liability. And then she would leave it all to the next generations. It was a perfectly legit way to avoid a massive tax liability. Having told us this much, Cummins, who clearly did not know he had a couple of Bagehot Fellows in his class, thundered the single most useful line I heard during my entire year in New York:

"Now what would the *liberal press* do with that? They'd have a field day! But they'll never get it, because they're *not smart enough.*" At that point, I kept my head down and scribbled, while my fellow Bagehot, Pam Luecke, next to me, sort of leaned over and giggled. When I looked up, I noticed one of the MBA students I was friendly with trying to catch my eye and smiling broadly. Professor Cummins was right, of course. Almost no reporters, certainly not me, understood the intricacies of how America's wealthiest families exploit the tax laws to their advantage. But now, at least, I was alert, and in my work as a journalist I would have a little more insight into how the system really worked.

I ran through my stipend by the end of April, as the fellowship year was winding down. The lease on my apartment at Columbia ran through May 31 so I resolved to give myself most of that month to enjoy New York before returning to Syracuse. I lived on my credit card for the final few weeks, going to plays and enjoying the city. I had some debt to pay off when I got back to work, but I never regretted a penny of it.

6

Inside the Pyramid

Toddlers who ask why over and over exhaust their parents. A reporter who asks why over and over does the necessary work of journalism.

When I got back to Syracuse following my fellowship in the spring of 1987, I was ready to find my next job with a newspaper in a bigger market. My job hunt would take me about six months (more about that in the next chapter). But before I left Syracuse, I worked on one final big project for the *Post-Standard*, one that amply rewarded this journalist's ability to keep asking.

Syracuse was the hometown of a businessman named Robert J. Congel. Then in his early fifties, Congel had started his career laying sewer pipe in Syracuse with little more than a pickup truck and work boots. But he invested his early profits in real estate development and muscled his way into the big-time world of shopping malls. As I write this in the early 2020s, online shopping and other trends have killed weaker suburban malls and upended the nation's shopping habits, so it may be hard to recall how in post–World War II America the enclosed suburban mall surrounded by a sea of parking came to dominate the retail world. Hundreds of shopping malls dotted suburban landscapes coast to coast, accelerating the decline of central cities and promoting consumerism as Americans' favorite pastime. Congel called his company Pyramid to denote solidity and permanence, and in the years before I started looking into its operations Pyramid had built major malls in several communities across Massachusetts and New York.

Along the way, Pyramid gained a reputation for sharp-elbowed relentlessness in pursuit of building its malls, a willingness to do whatever it took to achieve its goals. Most notoriously, in 1985 after the town board in Poughkeepsie, New York, had rejected Pyramid's application to build the proposed Poughkeepsie Galleria mall out of concerns for what it would do to traffic and traditional downtown retailers, Pyramid secretly bankrolled several pro-mall candidates. They were elected to the board and reversed the decision; when word got out it caused a scandal but the mall got built anyway. Pyramid batted down objections to its draining of wetlands at its chosen sites by building artificial drainage ponds; worries over traffic congestion could be overcome by building new ramps and bridges that Pyramid would pay for; to gather community support for proposed malls, the company sponsored letter-writing campaigns and blocks of broadcast advertising and shuttles that bused hundreds of residents from one community to its malls elsewhere to show off their appeal.

The average planning cycle took five years as Congel quietly bought up land before surfacing with a public announcement of their intentions. All this prep work cost money, millions of dollars, and often took years before Pyramid was able to start construction. The campaigns never slackened, no matter the opposition. "It's naïve to think you can coexist with those people," a former mayor of Ithaca, New York, was quoted in my story as saying. "The mall people work 24 hours a day to eat you alive." A Worcester, Massachusetts, business publication once described Pyramid's young and eager MBA-wielding team as "Beaver Cleaver without the self-doubt."

And now, in that spring of 1987, Congel and Pyramid were proposing to build their greatest creation on the northern edge of his hometown of Syracuse, replacing the tank farm known locally as Oil City along the shore of Onondaga Lake with Congel's biggest and most expensive mall. Downtown retailers were aghast. Fearing that Congel's mall would suck the life out of downtown, the debate became the big business story of the day. Congel himself and his company, built in his likeness, were almost preternaturally averse to publicity, Congel himself never giving interviews and all his mall projects fronted by younger aides who became the face of a project so that Congel's name seldom surfaced. I found the challenge of unlocking their secrets irresistible.

Like any deep-dive investigative project, I started at the outside and tried to work my way in. Congel himself either didn't respond to my requests for interviews or declined them, but gradually from public records and many interviews with others I built up a picture of his wealth and influence. Pyramid itself was headquartered in Syracuse's former downtown post office, a building that Congel and his wife redecorated with museum-quality art and vintage Oriental rugs and the latest in communications technology, including a boardroom where the yawning conference table was fitted with speakers so that Congel could hold his morning meeting with his teams at mall sites across the Northeast. Even more impressive was Congel's two thousand–acre wildlife preserve and lodge outside Syracuse, where he was planting thousands of trees and which he roamed in an old truck. An avid hunter, Congel featured many of his game trophies in this lodge, a caribou he shot near Hudson's Bay, an elk he took in the Rockies. All this I got to see in person when Congel finally relented and agreed to meet with me and a photographer at his preserve. So impenetrable had been his screen of privacy in the months leading up to the lengthy interview that I remember my editor shot me a look of relief when I returned to the office alive afterward, as though I had been lucky to escape—a bit of the paranoia that investigative journalism sometimes produces.

But through all this, the question of why Congel and Pyramid went to such lengths to overcome opposition to the mall projects nagged at me. To make a profit, sure, since malls were obviously packed with shoppers; they had become America's new town squares. And Congel was a stubborn man, not given to backing down from a goal. But winning approval for his malls often took years and cost Congel many millions in upfront costs for projects that may or may not come to fruition. Pyramid's relentlessness struck me as odd, or at least in need of an explanation.

Then there was a conversation I had with Congel's longtime friend and mentor, a man named Len Leveen, who with no fixed duties served as sounding board for Congel's ideas. Once Congel agreed to let his team talk to me, Leveen explained to me the ethos of a developer—a man who took worthless dirt and gave it value, he said—and he explained that he coached Pyramid's younger team members that anyone opposing their projects was "your enemy," and it was their job to overcome that enemy, be it an environmentalist or a downtown retailer or a city official. This righteous us-against-the-world approach struck me powerfully, indeed has stayed with me to this day, but it also left me wondering why the Pyramid crew and their founder Congel were so driven.

So throughout that summer back in Syracuse, as I circled around Congel until he finally relented and invited me to tour his wildlife preserve and talk about his work, I was trying to understand the heart of his finances. As many have noted, journalists don't have subpoena power like government prosecutors do; all we can do is look for public records and ask people for their help. As I slowly built up my narrative of his rise from pipe-layer to one of America's mall kings, I kept seeking the kernel of motive underlying the drive.

And then it became clear. There was no Deep Throat moment, no clandestine meeting in a parking garage; just that by continually asking the questions I found a couple of industry insiders who explained how malls got financed. It worked like this: A developer like Congel would borrow money to build a mall, say, $25 million in a construction loan. Then, at the opening of the mall, he would obtain a "takeout," or long-term mortgage, to pay off the construction loan. But the amount of long-term mortgage would always be much more than the construction loan, perhaps twice as much, because the amount was calculated not on what it cost to build the mall but on the value of the rent paid by retailers over the years to come. This "rent roll" could be calculated with precision for as long as ten years out, and since retail space in major malls was in such demand, rents paid by retailers were steep and increased year by year in preset leases; there could even be percentages of sales by the mall's individual retailers that would accrue to the developer as well. A mortgage lender wasn't lending based on the value of the bricks-and-mortar building but on the future value of that stream of rent payments; indeed, a mall at its most basic was a machine for generating revenue from rent payments. So a mall developer like Congel might construct a mall for $25 million and then get a $50 million or $60 million permanent mortgage. He would have to pay it back over years, but with rent revenue rising toward the sky that would be no problem, and because it was a loan rather than net income, he wouldn't have to pay any income taxes on it. In the meantime the developer could take those extra millions and do what he wished with them. A firm like Pyramid could pocket those surplus tens of millions, make its owners rich, and bankroll its next project in an ever-expanding pyramid of success. Not for nothing was the takeout known in the business as the "windfall."

Now the relentlessness of Pyramid's team became clear. Who wouldn't spend years and millions up front if the reward at the end was tens of millions of dollars in nontaxable cash? Congel's opulent headquarters, his vast wildlife preserve, his empire of malls across the northeast U.S., all were bankrolled by the ever-rising value that lenders and investors placed on shopping malls—on the malls and on the shopping habits of Americans who were abandoning older downtowns for the allure of the mall.

Overcoming all the opposition, Congel did build his mall in Syracuse, and he saw Pyramid through various ups and downs in the decades to come; he died in early 2021. His friend and mentor Len Leveen had died in 2018. I was moving on to my new job in Detroit as my big stories titled "Inside the Pyramid" ran in the *Post-Standard* in November 1987—a two-day series with extensive main stories plus sidebars. It was my most satisfying moment in journalism to that time. I suspect my year at Columbia thinking through tax problems and financing questions had primed me to see the importance of the gritty financial details. I finally felt I had the tools and insights needed to unravel for readers how this part of the world really worked.

*　*　*

There was one other lesson I took from my Pyramid project. At this stage of my career, I hadn't yet learned the importance of the *ending* of a story, what some call the kicker. Of course, I knew generally that an ending was supposed to deliver a final *oomph*, a moment of satisfaction and completion for the reader; but I hadn't yet seen the possibilities in my own writing. That changed when my editor, Mike Connor, made one crucial change in my draft.

I had set up my first main story in the two-day series as a history of Congel's rise, framed by glimpses of my experience touring his two thousand–acre preserve with him and our photographer. Amid the stretches of straightforward narrative of how Congel built Pyramid into a powerhouse, I offered anecdotes of him showing me around his preserve. I had planned the following little vignette as the *opening* to my story; Connor moved it to the end, and I saw immediately that he was right. For a story about one man's relentless rise and his unstoppable drive to build his malls against all opposition, this moment and the final line said it all:

> For 20 minutes, Robert Congel has been bushwhacking his 4-wheel-drive pickup truck through briars and wild grass, dodging evergreens and neglected apple trees. He stops, perched precariously on a hillside, peering out the driver's window at a trail snaking down the embankment. The road he hopes to reach lies in that direction, but the trail is far too narrow and steep to descend here.
>
> "Looks like an interesting ride down. What do you think?" he asks.
>
> From the back seat comes an uncertain reply. "Looks like there's a swamp at the bottom. . . ."
>
> Congel nudges the truck over and down they go. Tree limbs scratch angrily at the windshield. Leaves and twigs snap off and fly in the windows. The truck knocks low-hanging apples from the branches and they bounce off the truck like golf balls. But somehow, when the jouncing stops, the pickup is safe at the bottom.
>
> Once again, Bob Congel has gone where no one thought he could go.

7
Getting to Detroit

I had kept a journal during my year in New York, and reading back through it now in the 2020s, I see that in the second half of my fellowship year, the late winter and spring of 1987, I was preoccupied with thoughts of getting a new job. I could, of course, return to the *Post-Standard* in Syracuse after my fellowship, which I did, for a few months as it turned out, to write my *Pyramid* project, but I still hoped to move up to a bigger paper. I was enamored of the *Boston Globe* that year, as many young reporters were; something about the history and elegance of Boston attracted me. During my year in New York, I paid my own way to Boston and talked the business editor of the *Globe* into giving me a little time, although he could be no more than noncommittal about future openings. The *Washington Post* paid my way down to the capital for an interview, but no offer came from that either. The *Hartford Courant* called to ask if I was interested in editing their weekly business magazine, an intriguing idea, but I preferred writing to editing and they needed someone right away, which would have meant abandoning my fellowship, which was out of the question. The New York edition of *Newsday*, the Long Island daily, had me come in for a week-long tryout in their New York office in the spring of my New York year, a newsroom set high up in one of the chilly modernist office towers of midtown Manhattan, and while they were pleased with my work, I found the vibe a little odd. The editor there instructed me *not to take any other offers* without calling him first, but when I did get offers and reached out to him, he never returned my calls until after I had moved to a new job in Detroit.

I got to Detroit this way: Tom Walsh, the business editor at the *Detroit Free Press*, called me one day and said he had contacted Mary

Bralove, our Bagehot director, about that year's fellows who might be looking for a job. Mary pitched him on me as a candidate, and Walsh invited me to Detroit. I had never been to the city and didn't care about cars and the auto business at all, but something about the invitation intrigued me. An editor in Dallas, Texas, had called me about the same time, but I didn't see myself as a Sun Belt kind of guy. I preferred one of the older cities in the Northeast or Midwest, cities with a lot of history and culture—Boston, New York, Washington, Baltimore, Chicago, or . . . Detroit.

When I flew in for my interview at the *Free Press*, it was in late September, after I'd been back working in Syracuse a few months, and it turned out it was the very day that Detroit auto magnate Henry Ford II died, so my interview schedule got somewhat scrambled. I walked into the rather shabby business news section and saw one of those rubber chicken things hanging from the ceiling in the middle of the room. The editorial assistant, Harriet, just then dropped an f-bomb while talking about last night's hockey game. It was far removed from the formal and chill atmosphere I found in *Newsday*'s midtown aerie. Walsh and I hit it off, and when another editor took me out for a drive around town in a *Free Press* fleet car, the car ran out of gas and a *Free Press* tow truck had to come get us. They thought I would be appalled by such carelessness, but I found it all cheerfully informal, the town itself a mix of grit and hard work and a beautiful setting along the Detroit River with Canada just across the way. And best of all, they were looking for a writer to cover my emerging passion, urban affairs and economic development. It took Walsh a couple of months to come up with an offer, but I was glad to accept, and I moved to Detroit in November of that year, 1987. I was by that point thirty-seven and had been a working journalist for thirteen years.

The *Freep* hired a transport company to move my furniture, but I thought it best to carry a few things with me in my small car. I miscalculated how many possessions including clothes and my old TV I could stack in the back seat: my stuff filled my little vehicle top to bottom. Driving west from Syracuse, I took the Peace Bridge at Buffalo and cut across southwest Ontario to save time going around the long way via Cleveland and Toledo. When I got to the U.S. border at the Ambassador Bridge to Detroit, the U.S. Customs agent looked over my car, so crammed I could barely see out the back windows, and asked if I had anything to declare. I said "no." He waved me through. In those pre-9/11 days security was more informal. And that's how I arrived in my new city.

I had been at work in Detroit no more than a week or so when the editor from *Newsday* called to offer me a job in the midtown Manhattan newsroom. I would have loved to work in New York, but miffed at how he had handled it, I told him he was too late. Just as well. After a few years *Newsday* folded its New York edition, so by choosing Detroit I had avoided a layoff.

Like a lot of people who take a job in a new town, I remember thinking I'd give Detroit a couple of years and then move on. I certainly never thought I'd spend three decades and more in this city, not least because I didn't even care much about the cars for which the Motor City was famous. Nor did I know I would come to relish the chance to explore and write about the urban crisis from the most crisis-wracked city of them all. In short, I didn't reckon on how much Detroit would give me.

8

Detroit Free Press

In Detroit I met my wife, wrote my books, did the best work of my journalism career. It was here, thanks to my newspaper, I had the chance to visit so many other cities, each with its own story of stress and renewal. It was in Detroit I developed a theory of urban recovery in which the traditional sources of leadership—mayors, governors, the federal government—were less important than a mosaic of efforts by private and nonprofit actors, many of them working quietly in the distressed neighborhoods that had been abandoned by a car-crazy, suburb-bound America. In Detroit I could see new ideas of urban recovery germinate, grow, bear fruit, and inspire recovery efforts everywhere.

But that, of course, all took time. And if I write about the urban scene today with a good deal of clarity, I benefit from a lot of hindsight. I'd been hired by the *Free Press* to cover economic development, which in the late '80s in southeast Michigan meant covering the frantic, sprawling development of the suburbs, where new subdivisions and new office parks sprang up almost weekly. I wasn't seeing then the big picture of the urban crisis but only piecing together individual fragments as they came up day to day.

* * *

Eight Mile Road marks the border separating the city of Detroit from its northern suburbs in Oakland County. When I got to Detroit in the late 1980s, the communities north of Eight Mile were swelling with new residents and development. Homebuilders each year created thousands of new units, from apartments to McMansions. Office parks and retail centers were sprouting along the freeways.

Sports teams that owed their name and legacy to the city of Detroit were playing their games deep in Oakland County. Each year, bulldozers gobbled up yet more of the cornfields and orchards.

The story was much different south of Eight Mile Road. In the older city, population continued to drain away to suburbia. Company headquarters decamped to sunnier climes. Comerica, a bank headquartered in Detroit since Abraham Lincoln was practicing law, moved to Dallas. Poverty and joblessness, worsened immeasurably by racism and redlining, kept the city down. A few showcase projects, backed heavily by tax incentives, went up here and there, a skyscraper or two downtown, some gated communities along the riverfront. But the contrast was stark between the booming sectors to the north and the increasingly abandoned city.

The contrast formed the basis for a lot of my reporting in my early years in Detroit, in the late '80s and early '90s. So much was going up north of Eight Mile that I spent a lot of time covering projects in places like Troy and Novi, communities several miles north of the city. I wrote some as a reporter and others as a weekly columnist on economic development, and if my reportage was pretty straight ahead, in my columns I had the freedom to deride the wastage of suburban sprawl. I often belittled the notion that Oakland and Macomb counties could prosper by ignoring the distressed city to their south. I must have laid it on pretty thick because I got a reputation as a suburbs basher among some suburban officials and homebuilders. I probably deserved it. I believed strongly in *cities*, not suburbs, as the engine of culture and vitality. Once I wrote a column about the near-north suburb of Southfield trying to retrofit its sprawling low-density landscape with an instant "downtown." I offered this mocking assessment:

> My guess is that the new suburban "downtowns" will get it wrong. They'll create a few dozen boutiques, built in cutesy faux-Colonial style, surrounding a plaza deserted at all but lunch. It will be a museum diorama of a downtown. Out back, the expressways will continue to roar.

And when the Michigan Department of Transportation finally completed the central portion of the crosstown I-696 expressway, providing a high-speed route along that suburban corridor north of Detroit, I chided the celebratory fanfare that proclaimed that *East was meeting West!*

> Am I the only curmudgeon who declines to celebrate the opening of the final leg of I-696?
>
> Sorry, folks, but amid the hoopla, nobody mentioned all the damage that expressways have done over the years to our urban fabric. . . .
>
> There's no explanation for a policy that continues to create highways year in and year out, while public transportation systems atrophy. But it may help to recall the words of architectural critic Lewis Mumford, who wrote in 1958:
>
> "The current American way of life is founded not just on motor transportation but on the religion of the motorcar, and the sacrifices that people are prepared to make for this religion stand outside the realm of rational criticism."
>
> I-696?
>
> Bah, humbug!

* * *

When the market crash of the late '80s put a stop to the runaway suburban development (thanks to the debacle of the savings and loan industry implosion) I could turn my attention back into the city itself. Almost immediately I joined a team with reporters David Everett and Teresa Blossom to do one of the first computer-assisted reporting projects looking at racial lending patterns in Detroit. The *Free Press* got copies of government records collected under the federal Home Mortgage Disclosure Act, showing the raw data reported by lenders, these records on old-fashioned drum-type computer tapes that we ran on the newspaper's upstairs mainframe. Our analysis showed that banks and savings institutions routinely underserved even middle-class Black neighborhoods in Detroit compared to the loans they made in white districts. The effort involved a lot of door-to-door interviewing in Detroit neighborhoods. We spoke with Detroit developers attempting to do projects in the city who found themselves turned down by major lenders. The *Free Press* called the three-day series "The Race for Money." The series, published in mid-1988, made a huge splash and shamed the region's bankers into doing more, and I got to enjoy the glow cast on white liberal journalists when they're told they've advanced the cause of racial justice.

Earlier I quoted my favorite passage about journalism, from Mark Twain's memoir, *Roughing It*, about his youthful adventures in the frontier West. He was still young Sam Clemens then, trying to find himself in the silver mining boomtown of Virginia City, Nevada. Failing as a prospector and burning with ambition, he talked himself into a job with the local paper. And his boss explained that a journalist should go everywhere, talk to everyone, to get his story.

That's what I did in Detroit. And doing that, I saw what even the densest newbie could not miss—the overwhelming evidence of what white racism had done to Black Detroiters. There were the historic wrongs, including the destruction of the Black Bottom and Paradise Valley districts in the 1950s and discrimination in the auto industry. There was the failure of program after program of revitalization, well meaning but ineffective. There was the abyss-sized contrast between the schools available in upscale mostly white suburbs and those in poor Detroit districts. There were disparate outcomes in how police treated whites and Blacks, and there was the lack of jobs and financial credit available in the city. Everywhere the results of disinvestment and racism were plain to see.

The question for a journalist was how to write about it. Our "Race for Money" series had been a good start. But there was so much more to say—even if not all readers wanted to hear it. This was an early lesson in how, for a well-meaning white liberal reporter in Detroit, writing about race could be tricky. Black residents of the city accused the newspapers, even my progressive *Free Press*, of either ignoring the problems of poor residents or taking the side of mostly white developers and business leaders who were "revitalizing" the city in the probusiness, neoliberal belief that a rising tide lifts all boats. On the other side of the racial divide, many white residents of the suburbs thought we journalists were too quick to see a racial subtext to any story. At times it seemed nobody was happy with us, and perhaps with good reason. We knew, or should have known, that the *Free Press*'s own efforts to write about race with fairness and insight were hampered by the paucity of Black journalists on our staff. This became even more difficult after the 1995 newspaper strike in Detroit that saw leading Black journalists like Susan Watson leave the *Free Press* never to return. Well-meaning white liberalism can go only so far.

But as difficult as taking on race might be, it remained our urgent task, especially for those like me whose beat was the city. And there *was* a racial subtext to almost any story. I couldn't write about housing in Detroit without writing about how Black homeowners suffered far out of proportion to whites in the foreclosure crisis and Great Recession. I couldn't write about schools without pointing out the historic deficits in support provided for Detroit's mostly all-Black schools. I couldn't write about health care or unemployment or entrepreneurship in Detroit without considering race. And I couldn't cover all the new developments in Detroit without seeing how many developers wanted to turn a small corner of the city into some version of white, upper-class, suburban Birmingham; these projects provoked endless debate and recriminations.

A grim milestone: On November 5, 1992, I returned to the *Free Press* newsroom after an interview to find my colleagues gathered around the TV sets, the way they always did when big news was breaking. I saw my colleague Bill McGraw at his desk and asked him what was going on. "Two white cops beat a Black suspect to death with flashlights," he said. It was the infamous Malice Green case, where two white police officers did indeed pummel a drug suspect to death during an attempted search and arrest. When I heard Bill's words, my heart, my shoulders, my spirits all sagged. Any thought that we were making progress toward closing Detroit's racial divide evaporated in that moment. The Malice Green case, like the O. J. Simpson trial of a few years later, exposed the raw nerve ends of how race is lived in America.

Progress has been made, but as the George Floyd case in Minneapolis much later showed, America still has a long way to go to achieve racial justice. In my last few years at the *Free Press*, an anonymous caller occasionally left a message on my voicemail. The caller would leave his message late at night when I wouldn't be there to pick up the call, and I doubt he actually wanted to speak with me. Instead he filled the roughly two minutes available for each voicemail message with the most vicious racist epithets I had ever heard packed into a short time. The essence was that in my writing I, as a white man, was insufficiently loyal to my race. This guy left three or four of these messages over a couple of years. I could only hope there weren't many more like him out there.

So as a journalist I was schooled in the egregiousness of the problem and tried to get into the hard realities of how race was lived in my community. Over time, with layoffs within the newsroom and the loss of print ad revenue devastating the newspaper industry, our diminished staff struggled to cover even the most basic news, let alone the subtleties of race. As a columnist in my final years at the paper, I had the freedom to do more stories similar to what we tried to do with "The Race for Money." I'm sure it made a certain contribution. But in the end, no matter how in touch with urban realities I became, I saw that even informed and heartfelt white progressivism can go only so far. The *Free Press*, like so many other news organizations, simply had to hire more Black journalists. The *Free Press* tried mightily in this regard, starting with taking on a dozen or more interns and apprentices each year to groom our own talented journalists of color. But like so much else about how race is lived in America, these efforts could not disguise how much more we have yet to do.

* * *

There are perks and privileges to being a reporter on a first-rate newspaper like the *Free Press*, among them the invitations to participate in programs that took me across America and overseas. In the fall of 1989, the Robert Bosch Foundation, a U.S.-German cultural exchange entity, invited me to go on a sixteen-day visit to Germany. I had been at the *Detroit Free Press* a couple of years by this time, and I suppose the invite reflected my growing body of work on urban affairs. Our tightly scheduled visit would begin with a week in Bonn, which was then the political capital of the Federal Republic of Germany (or West Germany), where we would meet with politicians, professors, and other leaders. A few days in Munich would follow, then a visit to a small town near the border with communist East Germany, and our trip would climax with a final week in Berlin. No matter how the foundation had found me, I was happy for the adventure, and my editors and I worked out a series of stories I might file while in Europe.

What gave the trip piquancy were the political changes roiling the Soviet bloc. This was the era when the USSR's leader, Mikhail Gorbachev, had launched his twin policies of *glasnost* (openness) and *perestroika* (restructuring). Reform was in the air throughout Eastern Europe. By the time our small group (seven journalists from around the U.S.) arrived in Bonn, the rapidly developing events were already pointing toward a long-hoped-for opening of the Berlin Wall. The Wall had for a generation driven a fissure between West and East; it had become a symbol of the failure of communism to win adherents through free choice. Indeed, well over a hundred people in the East had died trying to cross the wall to the West and freedom. But the opening of the Wall was thought to be at least a year off, and the idea of reunification of the two Germanys was but a distant dream. As we began our visit, we had no idea events could move so swiftly.

Our pleasant first week in the West German capital had us staying at the Rheinhotel Dreesen, a beautiful and historic inn: Adolph Hitler had used it during his rise to power. We had a side trip to nearby Cologne, home to the best beer (known as *Kölsch*) I had ever enjoyed. Our schedule was full; it was my first visit to Germany and I saw that our hosts lived up to the image of Germans as Teutonically well organized; we had literally no time off. I was struck by the proficiency in English of everyone we met. We journalists, typical Americans, spoke not a word of German beyond *danke* and perhaps *guten Morgen*. I think it was here that I first heard the joke: If someone who speaks two languages is bilingual and someone who speaks three languages is trilingual, what is someone who speaks only one language? An American.

By the time we flew into Munich (as it happened, it was my fortieth birthday, and the weather was so touchy that we almost had to divert to another airport) the political situation had leapt far ahead. The Berlin Wall was opening; a tidal influx of East Berliners would soon flood the more prosperous half of the city for shopping excursions; a political revolution, bloodless and triumphant, was underway. And we were in the middle of it.

If one only knows Berlin today, long after reunification took place, it's hard to recall the grim look of the city in the fall of 1989. The Wall itself ran as an ugly scar through the city; Checkpoint Charlie and the handful of other Cold War crossings still operated. West Berlin was a vibrant democratic island within communist East Germany. People quipped that the temperature dropped a few degrees when you crossed the Berlin Wall into the East, so chilling was the oppressive control.

My first night in Berlin I headed inevitably to the Brandenburg Gate, the symbol of the divided city, where President Ronald Reagan a few years before had called on Gorbachev to "tear down this wall!" Multitudes gathered at the gate, anticipating the opening; television crews from around the world trained their cameras on the famous landmark; and as I stood there, I reflected that for the first time and perhaps only time in my career I was standing at the center of the greatest story in the world.

The opening of Brandenburg Gate would take a few more months, until a fitting ceremony could be planned, but East Germans did flood the western half of Berlin through other crossings that weekend. The contrast with the smartly dressed Westernized citizens was striking. The East Berliners in their shabby clothes, some of them driving their noisy, smoky Trabants (a vehicle that would never pass environmental muster in the West), seemed touchingly rustic.

It happened that the U.S. ambassador to East Germany at that time, Richard Clark Barkley, was a Detroit native. And my editors arranged for me to do a phone interview with him. Because one couldn't call from West Berlin into the communist eastern half of the city, I could only make the call from somewhere in East Berlin. My group of journalists had interviews scheduled in East Berlin that afternoon, and after we had done those the rest of my group left while I stayed behind to make my call at the appointed hour. I used a pay phone in a café. The ambassador was charmingly informal about it all; we talked about how he had bought his wife a Ford Mustang and how it had turned heads in the communist half of the city when she drove down the Unter den Linden. I gathered my notes (my story would be datelined *East Berlin*) and slowly walked back through the darkening streets to the sole elevated train stop where one could travel back into West Berlin. I would have been less than human to not feel I was walking in a John le Carré novel. At the train station I got in the wrong line and a burly East German cop gruffly ordered me to where I belonged. As our train passed over the no-man's-land on the communist side of the Wall, I thought the hideous zone was as grim a sight as I had ever seen. The temperature did indeed seem to rise a few degrees as we passed again into the West and into a free city.

Like thousands of others, I chipped out a few bits of the Berlin Wall for souvenirs, and stashed copies of German newspapers announcing the Wall's opening in my suitcase. I had a head cold by the time I got home to Detroit, but the adventure was worth a case of the sniffles.

I've been back to Germany a few times since then, either on reporting trips or vacation, as well as to many other European cities and countries. But I don't think I ever again had that feeling I had at the Brandenburg Gate that first night in Berlin, of being in the one spot on earth that the entire world was watching.

*   *   *

Reporters write a lot about violence. Whether in wars or crime, violence fills the airwaves and newspaper columns on a routine daily basis. Back in my City News Bureau days in the 1970s, I did my time on the midnight police beat and covered dozens of murders and other acts of violence in Chicago. But reporters, like the police themselves, almost never *witness* violence taking place. They show up only after the guns have done their damage. Usually, that is.

In the fall of 1990, a local train buff named Bob Cosgrove called me at the *Detroit Free Press* to invite me to visit the Michigan Central Station with him. Detroit's historic train depot southwest of downtown had once been the gateway to the city. Built in 1913, it was the tallest railroad station in the world and played a starring role in the life of the city. Uncounted thousands of Black sharecroppers and Appalachian whites had arrived there on their way to Mr. Ford's factories, and during World War II many a sad farewell or joyous homecoming took place there. As the nation's train service withered, the cavernous depot saw less frequent use, and finally Amtrak ceased running trains at the station in 1988. All this I knew in my job at the *Free Press*, and I knew that a suburban real estate broker and investor named Mark Longton Jr. recently had obtained title to the depot. I hadn't met Longton and was yet to hear his plans for the station. So I agreed when Cosgrove, a train enthusiast, suggested we visit the station and see if we could learn what Longton had in mind for it.

By then a chain-link fence surrounded the property, and Cosgrove and I were standing on the outside, trying to see what we could see, when Longton came out to speak to us. We stood a few feet apart on opposite sides of the fence. He struck me as tense, perhaps suspicious of who we were and what we wanted. Dressed for business in sport coat and tie, he was about forty, white, and looked slightly uncomfortable in his attire, as though his tie was knotted too snugly. He gave terse answers to our questions. I'm not a journalist who thinks he can read minds or size up a personality in a glance, but in the trade you do have to read a situation fairly quickly, and the word "tight" best describes the feeling I was getting off him. But that in no way explains what happened next.

Without warning Longton, spying a couple of men trying to sneak onto the grounds about a hundred yards to our left, whipped out a silver .45 caliber automatic from the waistband of his trousers. "Get the fuck off the property!" he yelled to the men, punctuating his command with rapid-fire shots—*Bam! Bam! Bam! Bam! Bam!*—in their general direction. By instinct rather than any conscious thought both Cosgrove and I ducked low. Having a businessman I was speaking calmly with one moment blasting away with a handgun the next moment was as freaky and as frightening an experience as I'd ever had in the nearly twenty years I'd logged in journalism.

Longton himself didn't seem fazed, and indeed the gunplay seemed to loosen him up. Reloading, he returned the gun to his waistband and told us the depot had been broken into repeatedly since he bought it several months earlier.

"I never owned a gun till I bought this place," he said. "It's like World War II out here." And having loosened up that much, he relented all the way, opened the gate for us, and proceeded to spend the next hour showing us around the interior of the train station, all the while regaling us with his plans.

He envisioned reopening the depot as a casino—even though Detroit voters had rejected casino gaming in the city up to then. He confided he would invest at least $65 million and maybe more than $100 million to make it happen. He admitted he didn't have the money but made cryptic allusions to foreign investors in Hong Kong and elsewhere. His speech pattern had the same staccato rhythm as his gunplay.

"Once I program my mind for a concept, I don't think about it anymore. I go do it until it happens," he said. "I don't believe in hope and I don't believe in luck. That's for rabbits. I work seven days a week. I sleep only four hours a night. And I gamble only on real estate. But I'm a high-risk gambler."

As it turned out, he should have saved his money and his bullets. Unable to make a go of the massive depot, and reportedly failing to pay his bills, Longton owned the station only for a few years before Detroit's most notorious businessman, Manuel (Matty) Moroun, who also owned the Ambassador Bridge linking Detroit with Windsor, Ontario, bought the train station. Moroun let the station sit vacant and increasingly forlorn, stripped and vandalized repeatedly, until in 2018 the Ford Motor Company, in an act of civic commitment little short of miraculous, bought the train station from the Moroun family to turn it into a center for future mobility research.

I covered the long, sad, and ultimately redemptive story of the depot over the years for the *Free Press*. But it was that moment of freakish violence in 1990 that stayed with me. Longton's firing on a couple of would-be scavengers was so unexpected, so out of place, so outrageous, really. I had thought I was interviewing a businessman, but this businessman was something I was apparently unprepared for. No doubt the sudden gunfire erupting just feet away frightened me. But more than anything I was astonished. It taught me the freakish nature of violence. I'm sure survivors of the mass shootings that have come to scar so many American lives in recent years were equally undone, and worse, when the gunfire erupted.

Nobody was hit by Longton's gunplay. I thought for a moment that he might have been firing blanks, just to scare off intruders. But when Cosgrove's car began to act up later that afternoon he discovered a spent bullet in the engine compartment. A ricochet had clipped a hose. We were lucky it hadn't hit one of us.

Perhaps most astonishing, the gunfire brought no response from anyone else. The cops didn't show up. Nobody did. True, the train station sat in a mostly vacant area of southwest Detroit, and I suppose it's possible that the firing went unheard and thus unreported. But it may have been Detroit doing what Detroit did then, ignoring the sound of gunplay at high noon.

*   *   *

Another bit of advice Mark Twain recalled from his early newspaper boss had to do with the tone to take in his stories.

> Never say, "We learn" so-and-so, or "It is reported," or "It is rumored," or "We understand" so-and-so, but go to headquarters and get the absolute facts, and then speak out and say "It is so-and-so." Otherwise, people will not put confidence in your news. Unassailable certainty is the thing that gives a newspaper the firmest and most valuable reputation.

It's good advice, but it also highlights the debate over what some call "moral clarity," the choices that journalists make about what to cover and how. The decision to go after a story, for one thing, makes a value judgment about what's important. Twain's editor articulated another value, the reporter's relationship to the reader. Whether that should always take precedence is open for debate, and is debated. Journalism has always kept one eye on the news and the other on itself.

My profession's relentless self-examination sometimes draws the notice of the wider public. Back in 1978, when I was working at the City News Bureau, the *Chicago Sun-Times* pulled off one of the great journalistic stunts when it set up a bar, appropriately called The Mirage, to see which municipal inspectors and regulators could be bribed into overlooking code violations. The twenty-five-part series made for riveting reading each morning. But the debate over the ethics of entrapping low-level inspectors and regulators through deceptive means cost the newspaper a likely Pulitzer. And it meant that the Mirage episode would always carry a stain, however much many of us enjoyed the series. In 2002 and 2003, Judith Miller published articles in the *New York Times* that confirmed Saddam Hussein was amassing weapons of mass destruction in Iraq. Officials in the George W. Bush administration eager to launch the invasion of Iraq cited her articles. When no such weapons were found and Miller's reporting was discredited, the public wanted to know how the esteemed *Times* could have been so credulous.

In 1990 the writer Janet Malcolm published her book *The Journalist and the Murderer*, which took up the question of the ethical responsibility reporters have to their sources. She offered this pugnacious assessment: "Every journalist who is not too stupid or too full of himself to notice what is going on knows that what he does is morally indefensible. He is a kind of confidence man, preying on people's vanity, ignorance, or loneliness, gaining their trust and betraying them without remorse." To support this baleful judgment she examined the interplay between writer Joe McGinniss and convicted murderer Jeffrey MacDonald, an Army doctor and former Green Beret who is still serving life terms for killing his wife and two little girls at the Ft. Bragg army base in 1970. MacDonald's defense team had enlisted McGinniss to sit in and observe their strategy sessions, expecting him to write a true-crime narrative exonerating MacDonald. But McGinniss quickly came to see overwhelming evidence of MacDonald's guilt, and rather than abandoning the defense team, he stayed with them and wrote *Fatal Vision*, his gripping narrative of the case that left no doubt that MacDonald had indeed killed his family. (MacDonald has lost all subsequent appeals.)

Malcolm took McGinniss to task for stringing his subject along. I and many other journalists disagreed. I thought then, and think so today, that Malcolm mistook the key relationship in journalism. That relationship is not between the reporter and the subject but between the journalist and the reader. I owe my readers my best, my most honest reporting of any subject I'm working on; if I bruise some feelings in the process, that's the nature of public discourse.

When I'm writing an article critical of someone, I owe the subject the courtesy of asking all the tough questions, so they at least know what's coming. But beyond giving the subject a chance to respond and being honest with them, I owe the subject nothing more. To the reader I owe everything.

While the Janet Malcolms of the world may say that the "reader" is a mere abstraction, I can testify to the opposite. During my years at the *Free Press* I met my readers every day on the streets of Detroit or heard from them in letters and phone calls or by email. Sometimes they liked what I'd written and told me they were informed or enlightened by it; other times their criticism of my work was scathing. But how useful would I be to my readers if I soft-pedaled my reporting to please the subject? McGinniss did eventually confront MacDonald with what he'd learned—on camera on *60 Minutes*—and that was indeed an ambush interview. But getting at the truth of what MacDonald had done to his wife and daughters justified that sleight of hand, at least in the minds of McGinniss and *60 Minutes* producers. And I have to say I agree.

As I write this in the early 2020s the world of journalism once again faces more soul-searching. In May 2020 an African American resident of Minneapolis named George Floyd died in police custody after an officer knelt on Floyd's neck for nearly nine minutes to restrain him, despite pleas from Floyd that he couldn't breathe. When a bystander's video went viral, the outrage over the officer's disregard for Floyd's distress even while being videoed shocked the world and led eventually to the murder conviction of the officer involved. The Black Lives Matter protests spawned by the incident focused on banning chokeholds and other forms of brutal restraints. But the protests also came to spotlight what many Black journalists and community leaders saw as a journalistic establishment that was dominated by whites, where a white middle-class perspective was taken as normative and where Black residents were seen mostly, if not exclusively, through the lens of crime stories. Many demanded that media outlets hire more Black journalists, a reform I totally support; even at the *Free Press* in Detroit, a progressive newspaper in a majority Black city, journalists of color were underrepresented in our newsroom.

But when journalist Wesley Lowery wrote an op-ed in the *New York Times* calling for more "moral clarity" on the part of journalism when it came to race, the self-assessments grew agonizing. Many worried that "moral clarity" meant abandoning traditional ethics of accuracy and fairness in favor of outright advocacy. What did Lowery himself mean by it? As he put it: "We also know that neutral 'objective journalism' is constructed atop a pyramid of subjective decision-making: which stories to cover, how intensely to cover those stories, which sources to seek out and include, which pieces of information are highlighted and which are downplayed. No journalistic process is objective. And no individual journalist is objective, because no human being is."

And with that I totally agree.

But here I must assert that we journalists can still live up to our core tenets of fairness and accuracy even while expanding our universe of subject matter and sourcing. As press analyst Tom Rosenstiel put it in his Twitter comments on Lowery's piece, nobody suggests "that [just] anything I am passionate about and believe deeply is a kind of real truth." Rather, as Lowery writes, journalists exercise judgment by selecting which stories to cover, and then they cover those with objectivity and fairness.

Take cop shootings. Too often journalists have taken the initial police account of a shooting as gospel. We now have seen too many cases where bystander videos reveal police misconduct. So in seeking interviews with other witnesses, in seeking out the friends and family of the "suspect" who was killed by police, journalists show they understand that official sources may not be telling the truth. But moral clarity doesn't mean we believe an account just because it differs from what the police told us. We still must test any and all versions against each other.

At the *Detroit Free Press*, I covered many topics that were not breaking news or likely to make splashy headlines. Topics like urban farming in the city's abandoned neighborhoods, or the rise of Detroit's small but promising entrepreneurial movement—these drew my attention even if they lacked the visceral punch of the latest political jockeying or economic upset. I chose to write about them because these stories, I thought, would give insights into Detroit's recovery efforts in a way writing about either crime or big downtown projects would not.

So in the selection of my topics I practiced judgment, or what I hope was a moral clarity about my city, trying to nudge the public debate in the direction I thought it ought to go. I don't know how anyone can work in journalism without making such judgments. But such necessarily judgmental choices didn't undo my commitment, or my ability, to strive at all times for objectivity and fairness.

*   *   *

An aside: Like many journalists, I have been a pack rat, saving tons of material I had collected on stories against the day I would reach into my files and pull out some gems. It took me a long time to see I was filling up my files mostly to feel a comforting security that I wasn't losing track of anything. Eventually during my years at the *Free Press* in Detroit I realized that I didn't need to keep all the reports, articles, background notes, and so forth that clutter a reporter's desk and that seem so important at the time. We're journalists, not archivists. I saw this when I began to analyze where the information in my published stories came from. I saw that the information in almost everything I wrote came either from new reporting each day, including daily calls, interviews, internet searches, and reading just-issued reports, or from background material retrieved from a search of past clips in our newspaper library system. But almost never did I reach into the earlier reports and background materials I had been dutifully storing for years on my desk and in my file drawers. I learned I could easily empty out my files with little or no loss to my reporting or productivity. Today, with even archived reports and the like easily available on the internet, there's less excuse than ever for burdening your workspace with all that old stuff.

Sad to say this lesson never quite took. My desk remained one of the messier ones at the *Free Press*—not exactly a landfill like some others in the newsroom, but pretty bad. From time to time I would spend an hour or two trashing the older stuff, but it was like hacking away at fast-growing weeds. Only when I retired from the *Free Press* did I have the good manners to leave my area clean for the next guy; I housecleaned to the point of a blank desktop and empty file drawers.

Reporters with clean desks aren't necessarily more productive than those with messy desks, but I do think life is easier without all the clutter. The same goes for all the books and reports that I and many other journalists lined up on our desks. Some I used frequently—a Detroit street guide (in the days before we had GPS apps on our phones), the *Detroit Almanac* published by the *Free Press* to mark the city's three hundredth birthday in 2001, the AIA Detroit architectural guide I cowrote—but multiple reports on cities and economics, like corporate annual reports and the like, these I kept but rarely consulted; the important books in my field, like Caro's *Power Broker* or Jane Jacobs's *The Death and Life of Great American Cities*, I kept on my shelves at home. Are books and reports lined up on our desks there because we use them on a regular basis? Or do we keep them there to inspire us (not a bad motive), or (a lesser motive) do we think they make us look smart? As they say in architecture, sometimes less is more.

* * *

Given Detroit's distressed state, we liked to celebrate whatever city projects we could. The first new skyscrapers to rise downtown since the 1970s got a lot of play; so, too, did the expansion of the city's Cobo Center convention hall (now Huntington Place). In the early '90s I did a series following the construction of the One Detroit Center office tower, designed by Philip Johnson and John Burgee, and for a feature on the marble and granite I spent a few vacation days in Carrera, Italy, where the famous white marble came from. Having traveled so far for a story, I was worried about not finding anything to write about, but as my train pulled into Carrera I saw streams running down from the mountains flowing white as milk with all the marble dust. At that instant I knew I had something: I knew I'd find good color material. A day later I had traveled high up the mountain with the marble cutters and stood inside the cavernous carved-out interior of the mountaintop hollowed out by the marble trade. Reporting takes you to places almost no one else gets to go.

There were other positive local stories. A new subdivision called Victoria Park, built in a blighted east side district and the city's first new subdivision in decades, prompted headlines for months. But in general the development picture was grim. Poverty was rampant, unemployment high, educational attainment low. This was the era that gave rise to "ruin porn," the practice of photographers, usually from out of town, parachuting in to shoot the eyesores—abandoned buildings—and capture images of nature reclaiming vacant fields. Perhaps the low point was the case of Malice Green in 1992; as I wrote in the *Free Press*, the case exposed all of Detroit's woes and seemed to give the lie to any notion of progress on race or any other of our urban ills.

In these years, the late 1980s and into the 1990s, the city had simply ceased to offer opportunities to a majority of its residents. This left Detroit facing an economic crisis of appalling dimensions. Utterly dependent on its automotive industry, the city had no way to recover when German and Japanese competition slashed away the market share of the Big Three—General Motors, Ford, and Chrysler. Factories closed. Jobs disappeared. Thousands of the tidy wood-frame bungalows that served generations of factory workers fell into blight when their owners fled to the newer suburbs to the north. The bizarre practice of Devil's Night, when mischief-makers set fire to hundreds of buildings just before Halloween, became emblematic of the city's woes. As the population shrank to a third of its 1950s peak and the tax base all but vanished, the municipal bosses at city hall found no way to stop the flood of red ink drowning the budget each year. Detroit, the home of Motown music and the Ford Mustang and the modern American labor movement, the city that once reigned as the world's industrial powerhouse, the famous arsenal of democracy in World War II, now stood as the international symbol of rust belt despair. In virtually every metric—crime, poverty, school test scores, unemployment—Detroit stood alone at the wrong end of the scale. And in almost every other city in America, hard-pressed civic leaders, dealing with their own problems, consoled themselves with the thought, *At least we're not Detroit.*

* * *

And so I spent my first several years at the *Free Press* writing about booming suburbs and a distressed city, while in the background, like hints of a storm brewing several states way, we learned that labor relations were growing steadily worse between the several unions that represented workers, including my own union, the Newspaper Guild of Detroit, and the city's two daily newspapers, my *Detroit Free Press*, owned by the Knight-Ridder chain, and the rival *Detroit News*, owned by Gannett, these two represented by a corporate agency that ran the two papers under a joint operating agreement. The heart of the dispute was the feuding between the Teamsters-represented drivers who delivered the newspapers and the corporate owners. By late spring of 1995, the rumblings of trouble ahead were impossible to ignore. I attended my union meetings and voted with the rest to authorize our leaders in the Newspaper Guild to call a walkout if necessary. Nevertheless there remained an air of unreality about it all.

Reality would intrude soon enough.

9

Union Activist

There's a quip that was beloved of right-wing conservatives in the age of Reagan that a conservative was a liberal who'd been mugged. It mirrored the law-and-order rants of the day and implied that liberalism went only skin deep, a dilettante's affectation that wouldn't survive an encounter with harsh reality. Not true, of course, but it illustrates where the lines are drawn.

Back when I first became active in the newspaper union movement at the Gannett-owned Rochester *Democrat & Chronicle*, I developed my own variant on that joke: A union activist was a worker who'd been mugged by a corporation. I believe that many of my fellow journalists in Rochester would have been content to work their stories and leave financial matters to the company if not for the oft-bruising treatment meted out to staffers. The low pay, the mean-spirited evaluations, and the punitive assignments were all part of it. And it ran deep. Once I played a game of racquetball with an acquaintance from the other Rochester paper, the *Times-Union*, and from the moment we met in the locker room he complained nonstop of the wrongs he had suffered at the hands of his bosses. This outpouring of grievances continued at every break in our game, even between points, and it didn't stop in the locker room afterward until we said goodbye. I thought to myself that there was a guy who definitely needed to find a new job.

But he wasn't alone, and in my first years in Rochester, the late 1970s, when I hadn't yet given up on working for a Gannett-owned newspaper, I drifted into the paper's nascent union movement as a way to improve my situation. There was a chapter of the Newspaper Guild in Rochester, but we had not negotiated a contract with management in years; in the guild world we were at the margins, carried on the books but not much more. There were a couple of serious activists among us and a couple more who volunteered. We had none of the professionalism I came to expect later in the union town that Detroit was; we had no lawyer or professional advisers to help us, and some in our newsrooms thought the drive for a contract was no more than a platform for telling the bosses to go screw themselves. It was anything but promising, but by dint of organizing our members over many months, a time of widespread discontent, we succeeded in negotiating a first contract with Gannett. It met the barest of our goals, including a tiny across-the-board guaranteed raise for the first time, but it marked a big step forward.

Was I temperamentally suited to union activism—a rebel or do-gooder by nature? Perhaps. In my midtwenties, back in my City News Bureau days, I once started a newsletter for my fellow staffers as a discussion forum about our work. My editors resented it; another reporter told me he heard one editor complain, "Gallagher works for us. We don't work for Gallagher." And like many such newsletters it lasted only a couple of issues before fading away. But nonetheless it created a stir. One friend at City News, equally unhappy with the low pay and general abuse of staff, said over beers one night that the newsletter had been the outfit's first stirrings of a union movement.

Yet if my temperament opened me to consider union work, it wouldn't have happened without getting mugged by Gannett. When I got to Rochester, my first and primary grievance was getting stuck on the copy desk instead of the reporting job I had interviewed for. (As I mentioned, my "temporary" assignment to the copy desk lasted more than two years.) My resentment was no doubt compounded by the stress of endless night work, of my loneliness in a new town, and of the fear a young person feels as they near thirty that life is slipping away with not much to show for it. But my impetus to take on union work would never have blossomed into anything had my bosses not been so, well, Gannett.

It wasn't long after we won that first contract in Rochester that I jumped to the Syracuse *Post-Standard*, owned by the Newhouse chain. My new paper was a nonunion property where local management was more benign and where my editors treated me with respect; indeed, they were delighted to have me. Happy with this improvement over Rochester, I made no moves toward starting a union there. As union activists have long preached, an oppressive management is a union's best organizer. Only when I got to the *Detroit Free Press* in 1987, a union paper in the strongest of union towns, did I volunteer again for steward training. I had no expectations or desire to become a union leader; I just found the ins and outs of contract work interesting and I enjoyed the camaraderie of union work.

The test of how deep my union predilections went would be settled only in 1995. On a muggy July evening with thunderstorms brewing, I joined twenty-five hundred other newspaper workers belonging to six unions as we walked out of the *Free Press* and *News* in what became Detroit's most protracted and most infamous newspaper strike. I didn't know it then, but those first steps out of the building moved me irreversibly into union activism in years to come.

10

On Strike

There's that scene in *The Godfather* where jolly Clemenza tells Michael Corleone about gang wars. A new one is about to start.

"We're going to catch hell," Clemenza says.

"How bad do you think it's gonna be?"

"Pretty goddam bad," Clemenza says, but then shrugs it away. "That's all right. These things gotta happen every five years or so. Ten years. Helps to get rid of the bad blood."

I'm sure more than a few of us thought of that scene on the evening of July 13, 1995, as we walked out of the *Detroit Free Press* and *Detroit News* buildings on strike. The older veterans of the papers remembered the nine-month Teamster-led strike in the late 1960s that shut down the papers, and there had been a one-week strike in 1980. But most of us had never walked a picket line before, and we thought—naïvely as it turned out—that we were embarking on a gutsy but probably short-lived demonstration of our resolve, a way to clear the air, to rid the system of bad blood, whatever that might mean. Some even thought it a lark. At our final prestrike meeting when we took the vote to authorize a walkout, the chair called for those in favor. Some six hundred journalistic voices thundered "Aye!" as one.

And so the strike began, just as a thunderstorm swept through the city. The immediate flashpoint was a refusal at the Gannett-owned *Detroit News* to rescind its insistence on, for journalists, merit raises only, that is, a refusal to offer annual across-the-board increases for all newsroom workers represented by the Newspaper Guild. Merit pay is inherently subjective, beset with problems of favoritism, and at Gannett the merit raises tended to go to only a few. The union's position was that across-the-board raises of even 1 to 3 percent a year allowed workers to stay abreast of inflation and recognized that all workers contribute to a paper's success. The unions had no objection to the companies giving merit raises on top of across-the-board increases, but merit pay alone was a bridge too far. Beyond that immediate flashpoint, the company hoped to break the power of the Teamsters union that controlled distribution of the newspapers.

Chris Rhomberg, a sociology professor at Fordham University, concluded in his book about the walkout, *The Broken Table*, that management provoked the strike and had been preparing for it for several years. My one-time editor in Rochester, New York, Robert Giles, now editor of the Gannett-owned *Detroit News*, was widely viewed as an architect of the company's hardline policy. And Gannett installed a man named Frank Vega on the business side to run the joint operating agreement. Vega was widely despised by the rank and file for his antiunion push; we called him Darth Vega. Both Giles and Vega were more than happy to go to war to break the power of the unions, especially of the Teamsters. But they underestimated how much pain the unions were willing to accept, just as the strikers miscalculated how much financial loss Giles and Vega could stomach to fashion the business model they envisioned.

A few of us picketed those first days at the distribution centers around town, where the papers fresh from the printing plant were off-loaded to deliverers. We couldn't block the entrances—the cops kept them clear—but we could picket and maybe yell a bit. One night, as the company mercenaries aimed a huge Hollywood searchlight directly at us, a striker held a full-length mirror to reflect the intense beam right back at them. If the goons could try to blind us, we could try to blind them. I suppose some thought it clever or good for a laugh; but I remember wondering how much you had to hate the other side to stand there with that mirror for half the night.

Besides setting up picket lines outside the downtown newspaper buildings the strikers also picketed the big printing plant complex in suburban Sterling Heights. With my friend and fellow business writer Greg Gardner, we joined hundreds of other strikers at the printing plant to picket. Once Greg gave me a bandana to cover my face in case we were teargassed. *Detroit News* editor Giles was determined to not let us disrupt distribution of the big Sunday edition, so he chartered helicopters to fly the papers out. We couldn't do anything about that except curse and jeer as the whirligigs lifted off every half hour or so with another load. Meanwhile, across the street from our picket line, the companies' hired goons and the Sterling Heights cops stood with their billy clubs, all too ready to bash heads if we gave them an opening.

We didn't stand alone. The United Auto Workers union banned the distribution of the *Free Press* and *News* in the auto plants. The UAW helped some strikers financially, organized protest events, and turned out their members to picket. Soon hundreds of rank-and-file members from many different unions were joining us on picket lines. Circulation and advertising boycotts were organized, and local political and religious leaders joined in our protests. Detroit remains the strongest of union towns, and so visible was the newspaper struggle that the UAW, the steelworkers, and other unions took up the strike as their own causes.

But a flaw in our strike strategy was evident right at the very beginning. A strike is effective only if it halts production. That never happened at the *Free Press* and *News*. The owners, Gannett at the *News* and Knight-Ridder at the *Free Press*, collaborated on anemic joint editions for the first few weeks of the strike. Those first papers were thin, ugly, and devoid of much good journalism, but they were on the street being sold, and in several weeks the companies had hired enough strikebreakers, both for the newsrooms and for the production facilities, to resume separate publication of the two papers. Our failure to shut down publication meant that the companies could ride out the strike, earning revenue from the advertisers and subscribers who remained. As Rhomberg writes in his book, "Workers and community residents showed an extraordinary solidarity with the newspaper strikers, in the largest popular demonstrations of labor support in the Detroit area in decades. Unfortunately for the unions, however, that support was still no match for the resources the papers were willing to devote to breaking the strike."

Rhomberg concludes that the unions, while making preparations, lacked any comprehensive plan for the strike, and the timing of the walkout was quicker than the unions wanted. He quotes John Lippert, my *Free Press* colleague who as labor writer had covered the newspaper negotiations before the strike, saying the union leaders were caught off guard. "The union leaders viewed the (strike) deadline as an impetus for intensified bargaining, and as a short-term response to anxious workers demanding some kind of action. They did not set it because they wanted a strike, or expected one, or had a plan for how to win it."

And we learned too late that our strike was never a traditional union-management dispute where two sides argue within the same conceptual framework. The unions thought they were fighting as multiple other unions in Detroit had for a couple of generations, jockeying according to established norms for a good contract. What they didn't realize was that Gannett, which called the shots in the dispute for both companies, wasn't playing that game anymore; instead, it was following, even pioneering, a new strategy to rid its workplaces of unions altogether. The taunting, mocking tone that company leaders like Giles and Vega took toward the strikers during the walkout revealed the contempt they felt for the traditional bargaining process overseen by the National Labor Relations Board. As Rhomberg writes, "One side comes to the table looking to make a deal. The other side comes looking to get rid of the table."

So despite the enormous financial losses the companies suffered, at some point it became almost business as usual at the papers, especially as the strike dragged on. A painful realization for me came when I saw that someone on the inside had taken our strike slogan "No Scab Papers" and mocked it with a "No Drab Papers" poster. The owners' resolve and indifference to the strikers' demands only grew in time, while the unions grew progressively weaker.

The strike was fought in the courts as well as in the streets. The six striking unions, including my Newspaper Guild of Detroit, filed unfair labor practice complaints with the National Labor Relations Board over the company's tactics. After extensive litigation the NLRB ruled in the unions' favor, potentially created a huge award of back pay for the strikers, but a federal court overturned the NLRB ruling and the strikers lost any hope of recovering lost wages. The companies, meanwhile, had fired many strikers for blocking entrances and similar activities, leading to yet more court battles.

Things could and did get brutal. Company security guards attacked and injured strikers. One example: On October 1, 1995, private security guards hired by the companies hit one union picketer, Vito Sciuto, on the head with a wooden stick, fracturing his skull and inflicting brain damage and other injuries that required surgery. I never witnessed such violence firsthand, but my guild colleague Daymon J. Hartley, a photojournalist, captured an infamous moment when off-duty Sterling Heights police lieutenant Jack Severance kicked a striking press operator, Frank Brabanec, at the printing plant while he was lying on the ground. In their turn, some of the strikers took to scattering "star nails" across the driveways of the printing plant or distribution outlets. These resembled a child's jumping jacks and they were designed to puncture tires of delivery trucks.

But there were lighter moments, too. One evening, having a beer at a local pub with other strikers, a Teamster gave one of these star nails to a woman striker he fancied. "Does this mean we're going steady?" she said.

So the strike did not end, as we had expected, in a few days or a week or two. It dragged on through the steamy hot days of that July and August and into the fall. And gradually some of the strikers decided they were too afraid of losing their livelihoods and crossed the picket lines to return to work. The best known was Mitch Albom, who I recall stayed out for seven weeks before returning; the unions never forgave him and some picketed his future book signings. The industrial unions in our strike, the Teamsters, printers, and others, grew disgusted that so many guild members were among those giving up and going back to work; one of their jokes was: "How do you reach a guild member? Dial 1-800-ICROSSED." Other strikers drifted away into new jobs and professions, a teacher here, a computer sales rep there. Our numbers and resolve remained strong for many months, but the slow drip of losses cost us.

In the guild we got strike pay of $100 a week, and I picked up enough freelance writing jobs to get by. Bob Berg, the one-time press secretary to Mayor Coleman Young, ran a p.r. firm then and threw an assignment or two my way. One was to promote a salvage scrap-yard in town that had crushers that could turn a car or truck into tiny shards of metal in mere seconds; that piece was worth a couple hundred dollars to me. Another friend had a business that produced training tapes for clients, and she asked me to serve as the voice actor reading training instructions for cashiers at Kmart. When I reminded her that I was not an actor and didn't have any voice training, she said the client wanted someone who sounded "real." So for a couple of hours one afternoon I voiced endless variations on: "If the customer presents a credit card, press tab A." I got paid a few hundred dollars for this effort. I only wonder whether my real voice was sufficiently reassuring to those Kmart cashiers.

When we at the unions launched our own strike newspaper, the *Detroit Sunday Journal*, I did almost all my strike duty there. I wrote angry editorials about the strike, did movie reviews and other stories, helped deliver the paper with a "walk and toss" on Sunday mornings. Working for a paper again, even a slim weekly, gave me a respite from the anguish of the walkout. For the first few months of the strike, I bitterly resented the companies' refusal to settle. But after that first Christmas, with my work at the *Sunday Journal* to fulfill me, being on strike simply became my way of life in Detroit. I stopped being angry or worried and simply did my *Sunday Journal* writing and my freelance work and enjoyed my hobby of sailing small boats on the Detroit River. Money was tight, but I got by. Many others suffered much more.

* * *

The time off during the strike did grant me one inestimable benefit. Enjoying sailing as much as I did, I volunteered to teach it at my club on Detroit's Belle Isle Park. And there, one May evening during the newspaper strike, the woman I would marry was in my assigned boat the first night of class. Sheu-Jane was then teaching bioengineering on the faculty at Wayne State University (she went on to a more entrepreneurial career in time). The sailing class continued all summer, and at one point another woman in the class told Sheu-Jane, "I think John *likes* you." Indeed I did. I asked her for a first date to our annual end-of-season banquet, and in time whatever mental block that had kept me single into my forties had happily dissolved. Sheu-Jane and I were married two years later.

* * *

The strike lingered until February 1997, when the unions, depleted by members who had crossed the line or drifted into other careers, with no end in sight to the struggle, made the unconditional offer to return to work. It was surrender in all but name. The newspapers, which had managed to publish during the strike by relying on nonunion editors and a lot of strikebreakers, said they would take us back but only as openings emerged, in effect turning the strike into a lockout; no way would they discharge the strikebreakers they had hired. The papers called us back by seniority, and my friend and fellow *Free Press* business writer Barry Rohan was the first to get the call. A few dozen of us accompanied him to the front door of the paper and cheered as he re-entered the building for the first time in nineteen months. My turn didn't come until that November. I had been on strike and lockout for two years and four months before I got my job back.

Why hadn't *I* crossed the line? Strikers had to answer that question for themselves. One older guild journalist who had been among the most vocal critics of newsroom management prior to the walk-out nevertheless crossed the line. On the other hand a woman who many in the newsroom thought might cross stayed on strike and became one of our most vocal supporters. For myself, I put it down to pure Irish stubbornness. But I don't think there's any facile explanation. Perhaps I thought staying out was heroic, a once-in-a-lifetime opportunity to take a stand that required real sacrifice. Then, too, my work at the *Sunday Journal* was satisfying, if not terribly remunerative. And I believed in the union movement and in the rightness of our strike, however much I came to see the folly of letting it continue as long as it did. Whatever the blend of motives, I knew there was no way I was going to cross the picket line and become a scab.

The newspaper companies, Gannett at the *Detroit News* and Knight-Ridder at the *Free Press*, suffered historic losses in the strike. Some estimates say the companies lost $100 million in the first few months. The companies had to spend a fortune on extra security and legal expenses. When it was all over and I had returned to the *Free Press* and was assigned to cover the dregs of the dispute, I asked Gannett's Frank Vega about it, and he told me the loss from the strike was $200 million (or about $325 million in 2020 dollars). And many among the public boycotted the papers and never went back. The catastrophic decline in circulation due to the boycotts was probably the worst pain we inflicted on the companies—at least two hundred thousand daily subscribers, about a third of the total, dropped the papers and never returned.

But the unions suffered, too, almost beyond measure. The Newspaper Guild took six hundred members out of the *Free Press* and *News* buildings, and by the time it was all over we had barely sixty striking members returning to the papers. The guild lost jurisdiction over staffers on the business side and of assistant editors in the newsrooms. The Teamsters, the largest of the unions, lost even more. The company slashed their delivery workers' pay, fired or laid off hundreds, and took the steps it wanted to replace well-paid distribution workers with independent contractors.

There are still conflicted feelings about it all, even a quarter century later. Many see the strike as a watershed moment when workers refused to "take any more." In this view our strike represented not only one industry but the labor movement taking a stand. And many believe there were groundbreaking political effects of the strike. In one editorial the newspaper companies threatened to move all operations outside of Detroit proper if City Council President Maryann Mahaffey, who had been leading resistance at the distribution centers, did not back off; that dispute raised the confrontation into the political arena. And no doubt the strike helped build the spirit of resistance in the community and within the broader labor movement. The strike increased participation in progressive movements of all kinds in Detroit. When leftists list notable "fight back" events of the last few decades, the strike is placed alongside the Battle of Seattle, Occupy, and now Black Lives Matter. As a friend and strike supporter told me, "Not too shabby for a defeat."

But those few dozens of us journalists who reclaimed our jobs and slowly rebuilt our union from within the newsroom take no celebratory view of the strike. As in *The Godfather*, the damage inflicted by this gang war could never be said to have been worth it. The pain inflicted on all sides—upon the unions, upon the companies, and upon the city of Detroit—proved greater than anyone had thought possible that first stormy July evening. But wars tend to do that. A quarter century on, I see the strike as a disaster for the unions and a disaster for the companies and a miscalculation on both sides that hastened the decline of journalism in a major American city. Surveying the wreckage from this distance, I call the strike a double suicide by the companies and the unions, a war where victory was indistinguishable from defeat.

11

The *Detroit Sunday Journal*

In late 1995, a few months into our newspaper strike, it became clear no settlement was near, and we in the unions began to produce our own strike paper to compete with the *News* and *Free Press*. The *Detroit Sunday Journal*, as its name implies, was a weekly, created by the striking journalists and production workers from the unions. Like other strike papers of yore, the *Sunday Journal* was a small paper that spoke with a feisty voice; and since the best reporters, writers, and photographers in Detroit were working for it (we earned our strike pay of $100 a week there instead of doing picket-line duty) the paper was filled with the best photographs, feature stories, and news writing in town.

Strike papers, while short-lived and of limited impact, have played an outsized role in the annals of journalism. Birthed in bitter labor disputes and created as a finger in the eye of the corporate owners of mainstream papers, strike papers have offered journalism laced with a bracing shot of defiance. There was the *Madison Press Connection*, formed in Madison, Wisconsin, in 1977 by union employees striking the town's two daily newspapers, the *Wisconsin State Journal* and the *Capital Times*; that one ran for three years. And in the 1930s, striking journalists at the Seattle *Post-Intelligencer* printed a separate paper of their own, the *Guild Daily*. Like the *Detroit Sunday Journal*, these strike papers punched above their weight, briefly hitting readership figures in the tens of thousands, and were ever after remembered with pride by the journalists who worked on them.

I wrote all sorts of things for the *Sunday Journal*, from news stories to rather angry editorials about our strike. But my main role, and an example of how varied a long writing career can be, was as one of the *Sunday Journal*'s two movie critics. What qualified me for such a role? Not a thing, except that when we were volunteering for jobs at the paper, I mentioned that I had always wanted to try it. To prepare, I tried to school myself in film history, watching old silent movies, Charlie Chaplin films, and foreign-language classics, all the while reviewing whatever Hollywood served up that week. I saw something like three hundred movies during my reviewing stint, sometimes two a day, occasionally at a regular theater with a preview audience but mostly during the day at a small viewing room in suburban Detroit with just a couple other critics (including the scab reviewer from the newspaper I was striking against). Among much else, I learned how many rotten movies are made. Seeing a pulpy, bloody exploitation film just after breakfast is not a great way to start the day.

Publicists lined up interviews for us, mostly with the B-list actors since the *Free Press* and *Detroit News*, which managed to continue to publish throughout our strike, were getting the A-list stars. But I also got to sit down with actors I greatly admired. I met with John Cusack to talk about his film *Grosse Pointe Blank*, and with one of my favorite British actors, Jeremy Northam, about his role as Mr. Knightly in *Emma*, and enjoyed a lunch with the great Stanley Tucci about his passion project *Big Night*, which remains one of my favorite films.

I shared the reviewing duties with another *Free Press* striker, Bill Hanson, and with our editor Gary Graff we devised a rating system based on three symbols: An arrow pointing up meant "See it now," an hourglass icon told readers to "Wait for the video," and an open book warned "Read a book instead." I saw many great films during the roughly year and a half I did reviews, like the Geoffrey Rush breakthrough film *Shine*, and waded through the trash, too. As one-time Hollywood star Ronald Reagan (whatever happened to him?) once said of his own films, they didn't want them good, they wanted them Thursday.

It was a pleasant enough way to spend a year and a half on strike duty. After many years of writing straight business journalism, I enjoyed the freedom of a critic's role that let me flex some new writing muscles and make some stabs at humor. Here's a brief sample from my review of the rather forgettable comedy *Father of the Bride, Part II*:

> The gag here is that affable George Banks, having barely survived his daughter's wedding in the 1991 film "Father of the Bride," must now confront becoming a grandpa at the same time his own wife gets pregnant again. Banks, played by Steve Martin, thus gets hit by a double whammy—too young to be a grandfather, but too old to struggle with diapers and baby puke all over again.
>
> Doubled pregnancies ought to dish up double the laughter, right? Perhaps, but director Charles Shyer keeps overloading his film with pieties. We can't just laugh at Banks' discomfort; Shyer wants us to go all soft and fuzzy about the possibilities of middle-age parenting. We haven't heard this many tributes to motherhood since the last Republican convention.
>
> Everything about the pregnancies is so perfect as to be slightly unreal. Martin and Diane Keaton as his wife want us to take seriously their angst over menopause and aging, but we're too busy admiring their dining room set. The new babies don't even cry in this film.

Writing was only one of my duties at the paper. Early Sunday mornings, I met two friends and fellow *Free Press* strikers, Rob Musial and Barry Rohan, at Barry's house in Grosse Pointe Woods. There we took a bundle of five hundred copies of the new edition of the *Sunday Journal*, folded them, and went on a "walk and toss" in one of the suburban Grosse Pointe neighborhoods. Afterward, we'd head back to Barry's house where his wife, Kathy, made us breakfast. We joked that we had all started our careers as paperboys and were all ending them the same way. One Sunday morning, ignoring a "Post No Bills" warning on someone's lawn, I tossed a *Sunday Journal* onto the porch anyway, and a tall, muscular, crew-cut homeowner, looking like an aging Marine, shot out his front door and headed my way. Naturally I picked up my pace down the street, and Rob Musial, with his genial personality, inserted himself between us and gently defused the situation. I didn't make that mistake again.

The *Sunday Journal* lingered even after the unions made their formal offer to return to work in February 1997, since the newspapers didn't take us all back at once but called us back one by one over time. But the slowly diminishing number of staffers made it difficult to keep the little paper going. It put out its final edition in 1999 after a four-year life, one of the longest runs on record for a strike newspaper. The full run of the *Detroit Sunday Journal* can be read in a digitized, searchable format at the Wayne State University Library.

For all of us who produced the *Sunday Journal* in those hard years, our work there remains a bright spot in the otherwise bleak landscape of the strike. For little pay, while dealing with all the emotional and financial baggage of being on strike, we produced some of the best journalism in Detroit. Looking back on my long career in writing and journalism, for me the *Sunday Journal* holds a very special place.

12

Newspapers in Transition

Like a man awakening after a long, long nap (Rip Van Gallagher?), I saw that two trends barely noticeable before our strike were growing increasingly visible in the years after I returned to the *Free Press* in late 1997.

One was the catastrophic decline of newspapers in American life. And the other, more happy, was the rise of creative strategies in rust belt cities like Detroit to reinvent themselves after decades of decline. I'll look at newspapers in this chapter, cities in the next.

For some time already, the worrisome trend, to those of us working in America's newsrooms, was the increasing transfer of ownership of newspapers from local, old-line family owners who nurtured their papers with a paternalistic attitude toward their communities to new owners, backed by big investment funds, operating as nationwide chains like Gannett. For these new owners, whatever bromides about public service they spouted, the bottom line was their overriding consideration. This consolidation into corporate chain ownership was designed to create powerhouse revenue generators that would wow Wall Street with ever increasing earnings. That the goal might be inconsistent with devoting resources to local coverage was papered over with encouraging press releases, but we saw the evidence as newsroom budgets began to tighten. It would take another decade at least after I got back from the strike before we saw that these engorged corporate entities—Gannett, Knight-Ridder, and the rest—were helpless before the inrushing tide of change.

Newspaper owners had shed their afternoon editions twenty years before, but now the annual Audit Bureau of Circulations releases showed the drip-drip-drip of declining readership even for the big morning dailies. The Detroit papers, of course, had taken a massive hit during the strike and never regained that lost circulation. But now the loss was accelerating as the new online world began to rattle us. Google launched in 1998, Facebook in 2004, YouTube in 2005, Twitter in 2006, with more to follow. While our core newspaper readership stayed with us, that readership was slowly "aging out," and the young, educated, upwardly mobile leaders of the future weren't buying or reading newspapers. I still recall the despondent feeling I got when a friend told me she got all the news she needed from Facebook.

If the loss of readers hurt, the loss of advertising revenue threatened the very existence of newspapers. That it came on gradually only made us like the metaphorical frog in the slowly heating water, not realizing its danger until too late. That we journalists all used Google, Twitter, and the other online venues in our daily reporting may have also shielded us from seeing the danger ahead. Slowly these online newcomers could offer advertisers reach and convenience that old-line newspapers couldn't. The classified ads in newspapers disappeared first, replaced by online offerings like Craigslist; this cost newspaper companies what had been an almost comically lucrative source of revenue. And the new online giants could target ads in a way general interest newspapers never could. As recently as 2005, newspapers as a group were still pulling in close to $50 billion a year in ad revenue. In the early 2020s, the figure is under $10 billion and still dropping.

The data from circulation figures was just as dispiriting. The Pew Research Center in its annual "State of the News" report notes that in 1990, weekday newspaper circulation was 63.2 million and for Sunday newspapers 62.6 million. By 2020, the combined print and online circulation of daily papers was 24.3 million and on Sunday 25.8 million.

With the drop in ad revenue and circulation, newsroom employment plunged, too. Pew Research, citing Bureau of Labor Statistics data, reports that about seventy thousand reporters, photographers, editors, and other newsroom staffers worked at U.S. newspapers in 2004; by 2020, more than half those jobs had disappeared and only about thirty thousand remained.

Our first big layoff at the *Free Press* came with the Great Recession of 2007–9. The paper let go nineteen of its staffers. It was a miserable day in our newsroom, but at least we still had enough of the old spirit to give good sendoffs, with tears and hugs and Irish wakes. At some point, I suppose, the steady drip of further layoffs came without so much ceremony. When I first came to Detroit in 1987, the *Free Press* carried about 320 people on the newsroom payroll—sports, features, the library staff, business news, city desk, photo, copy desk. We had a full staff of cultural writers covering dance, theater, books, and the like, a full library team to help with research, a full traditional copy desk. The *Free Press* when I first arrived in 1987 even had a nurse on staff; she warned me once in blunt terms that it was time for me to get my blood pressure under better control (I did). All these staffers vanished year by year into the memory hole. When I finally retired at the end of 2019, the *Freep* staff was under one hundred, and entire departments had been zeroed out or close to it.

* * *

Of course, back before all the layoffs began, before corporate owners began dismantling America's newspaper staffs and preaching the virtues of "doing more with less," we journalists never imagined we were living what in hindsight looks like the lush life. A generation ago in my newsroom of the *Detroit Free Press* (as I'm sure in all newsrooms everywhere) we always complained that we never had enough people to do all the work, and we grumbled that the space allotted for our stories was never as large as we wished to give our work the length it deserved. In the late '80s and into the '90s and early 2000s, grousing about resources was part of our daily dialogue on newspapering, a sort of verbal wallpaper always in the background.

What we wouldn't give to have those days back!

In a world in which corporations have cut not just the fat but the bone and sinews and heart out of our local newsrooms, some tales of that earlier extravagance have become legend. There was the investigative team for the Long Island newspaper *Newsday*, whose mandate was to go anywhere and take all the time they needed to win another Pulitzer or two. The leader of the team was a man named Robert W. Greene, and when he died in 2008 the *New York Times* obituary noted his expense-account tastes:

> Mr. Greene thought no expense should be spared in investigative journalism. As Anthony Marro, a former editor of Newsday, wrote in a 2002 Columbia Journalism Review profile of Mr. Greene: "The result was close to four decades of lobster dinners and two-inch-thick steaks, double Tanqueray martinis, and endless bottles of Pouilly-Fuissé and Châteauneuf-du-Pape. He once stopped a reporter new to the team from ordering a Salisbury steak in a restaurant, saying: 'When you eat with the team, you don't eat chopped meat'."

Well, we never ate lobster or thick steaks on duty at the *Detroit Free Press*, but some of the outlays even at the *Free Press* seem remarkable in hindsight. The *Free Press* once operated three foreign bureaus as part of the Knight-Ridder chain of newspapers, with a reporter in Africa, one in Eastern Europe, and another in Canada. These were expensive operations to maintain, but I never saw management flinch about expenses. Once, one of our reporters in Detroit put his name in for the opening in our Canada bureau. Since Canada is officially bilingual, this reporter told his editors they should send him to a French language school near Montreal for a few weeks to help him prepare. And the editors agreed. It didn't even seem that unusual an expense. Today those foreign bureaus are gone, victims of budget cutting. And sending a reporter to language school for a few weeks would be an indulgence of almost speechless profligacy.

We used to travel out of town for reporting trips with nary a peep from the front office. In the late 1980s, after automaker Chrysler had acquired the smaller AMC brand, Chrysler CEO Lee Iacocca broke his promise to keep AMC's Kenosha, Wisconsin, plant operating for several more years. The news of the plant closing broke in late morning; my editors told me to get my ass to the airport and get to Kenosha to talk to workers at the shuttered plant. I drove to Detroit

Metro Airport, ran to catch a flight to Chicago's O'Hare (they had to open the cabin door to let me on), rented a car, and drove up to Wisconsin. By early evening I had found a bar opposite the factory and enough angry workers to make my story. I'm not sure what that flight and car rental and overnight stay cost the paper—maybe the equivalent of about $1,000 or so today. But the question of cost never came up. The news came first.

Or there were our annual trips to the Mackinac Island resort, where the Detroit Regional Chamber gathered CEOs and Michigan politicians each spring for a four-day policy conference at the famous (and expensive) Grand Hotel. The *Free Press* used to send multiple staffers to cover the event—political and economic reporters, opinion writers, and top editors. In my first time covering the event (in the late '80s) our executive editor treated all of us *Free Press* staffers on the island to dinner the first night. I counted about fifteen of us at the table, including a couple of spouses who had come along. By the time I covered my last Mackinac conference in 2018, there were only four of us from the *Free Press* there and dinner was a beer and a burger on our own. The following year, my editor bluntly told me that I wouldn't be going to Mackinac that year for budget reasons. The idea that the newspaper didn't have the money to send its business columnist to the state's leading business conference said a lot about how much times had changed. Buyouts became an annual ritual, and "doing more with less" turned out to mean doing less with less.

One particular cutback pained me. The *Free Press* used to employ a full-time book critic who oversaw two full pages of locally written book reviews each Sunday and another page on Wednesday. The book editor had a private office lined with bookshelves and stacked with the cartons of new books that publishers sent us. Given my love of books and reading, it seemed like nirvana to me; being book editor would have been my ideal job. I never got to do that job, but I was a regular contributor of reviews for our book pages at $100 per review. The book editor's job disappeared in the downsizing; so, too, did the locally written book reviews and the three pages devoted to books each week. Doing book reviews had been a joy for me, and I was deeply sorry that I no longer had that outlet.

Over in my section of the paper, Business News, when we moved into new offices in 1999, we had four business editors, two editorial assistants, and about fifteen reporters. When I finally left the paper twenty years later, the Business News team had just one editor and another part-time editor, no editorial assistants, and only half as many reporters, all to report on one of the newsiest business towns in the country. Across the *Freep*'s newsroom, entire areas of coverage had been dropped.

The story was the same almost everywhere. At the *San Jose Mercury News*, a newsroom staff that peaked at four hundred journalists during the height of the dot-com boom had shrunk to a few dozen by 2020. The owners of the venerable *Cleveland Plain Dealer* all but dismantled its staff. At the *Free Press*, we lost two-thirds of our newsroom staff over those years.

What made this grim slaughter worse for those of us who carried on was that much of the public didn't seem to care. The rise of alternatives in the online world satisfied many. We newspaper reporters had always competed with television and radio news. But TV news never cut into our staffing levels at our papers, and besides, we print journalists could always feel superior to the fare running on local TV—and for the most part, the public seemed to share the sentiment. The competition from the online world and social media was different. People who took what passed for news on Facebook and Instagram and other digital offerings didn't seem to know or care what traditional newspapers provided. The once-proud profession of newspaper reporter was sinking into irrelevance.

Those of us lucky enough or with enough seniority under our union contracts to remain tried to carry on with our work, minus the out-of-town reporting trips and all the other things we used to take for granted. And, as always, we still grumbled about the dearth of resources. But a lack of resources was no longer just a background topic as we went about our business from around 2000 onward. It increasingly loomed as a threat to our way of life, and to the institution.

* * *

Now, even for someone like me, a lifer who couldn't imagine quitting the field, I had to acknowledge that the job wasn't a viable career for everyone. Nor was it ever thus. In the early years of my career, back in Chicago and in Upstate New York, our frequent, even nightly, bitch sessions took place over a few beers in any number of bars and pubs. Today, some four decades on, as I write this in the 2020s from my home in Detroit, I see that these reporter gripes about the shortcomings of a life in journalism have moved online. But from my reading of the complaints of young journalists in forums like X, the content remains much the same as it was in my day. Low pay, uncompensated overtime, overbearing editors, and limited prospects for advancement dominate the topics for young journalists now just as they did when I started my career in the mid-1970s.

Why, then, do journalists stick with it? The stark fact is that many don't. In 1990, I attended the one hundredth anniversary celebration of the City News Bureau of Chicago at a hotel ballroom off Michigan Avenue. Many of my contemporaries had already by that time quit journalism for other fields. The young woman who had shepherded me on my first day at City News was now an attorney; the best police-beat reporter I ever knew was selling real estate. Several others, I found, had gone to law school (for a low-paid reporter covering the courts, the lawyers in their suits, with their verbal finesse and the respect they commanded in court, made the legal profession look like an attractive alternative). Still more of my contemporaries had taken lucrative jobs in public relations. (A reporter in Rochester, New York, was asked why he had jumped from newspaper work to corporate p.r. His reply: "They doubled my salary.") Others had simply been unable to stomach the deadlines and general sense of being stepped on by editors. My rough estimate is that no more than half the younger reporters at City News in my days were still in the profession even these dozen or so years later.

Nor was the attrition rate much better at the most venerable institutions. Even at a major paper like the *Detroit Free Press*, where I spent thirty-two years as a writer, I saw many of my colleagues decamp for p.r. jobs. The University of Michigan hired so many Freepsters for p.r. roles that we began to quip that UM was our Ann Arbor bureau. The automotive giants, GM, Ford, and Chrysler, snapped up others.

Most discouraging, at least for those of us who spent our careers in newspaper work, was the high wastage rate among the youngest reporters. With so many online opportunities opening in the digital world by the third decade of this century, it was common to see talented twenty-somethings take their clips and their energy and enter another lane entirely on the digital highway, to leave newspapering far behind.

So I repeat, why did those of us who stayed, stay with journalism? No jokes here, nothing about how if we'd left newspapering we'd have to work for a living. A serious inquiry: What made me, in my late twenties or early thirties, bear with the long hours and low pay and the sometimes-humiliating dressing downs from editors to emerge with a career I could be proud of? What makes a journalist tick?

A stab at an answer: I suppose that all journalists enjoy, as I did, the sense of independence that comes with being a reporter. True, you are bound with chains to your editor's whims, but in a roomful of politicians or true believers of one stripe or another, reporters may be the only ones there with the freedom to think and speak their minds. An image once came to my mind of a military formation, troops shoulder to shoulder, alike as a row of pins, their commander the correct and proper number of paces in front, while off to the side, by himself, in his rumpled suit and slouch hat, stands the reporter. If this professional observer cannot order the "Charge!" or, in a courtroom, step up and take over the argument from a windy attorney, the power to take it all in and then go to the keyboard and send the story out to the world is a power unimagined by all the others. Seeing one's writing published under one's byline, with the responsibility that goes with it, more than makes up for the seeming lack of direct action.

Then, too, reporters bring two seemingly contradictory traits to their work. Many, like me, are essentially bookworms who read voraciously and haunt the shelves at the library or used bookshops; yet we are also outgoing, open to new experiences, intensely interested in the world at large. A newsroom is our natural habitat. Of course, new reporters must learn to handle themselves during an interview; going bellybutton to bellybutton with some powerful figure in the community can be intimidating. But those of us who made a go of it learned in the early years how to prepare, how to ask questions, how to emerge from a difficult interview with one's notebook full and one's dignity intact.

Some veteran journalists will tell you that low pay and brutal hours and scornful bosses have always been there, a rite of passage for journalists; and, they say, this new generation should put on its big-boy pants and stop whining about it. I don't buy that. I have nothing but sympathy and support for those who left the field early on. If I had had to work my entire career at the dismal pay and with the lack of control over my work that was mine in my early years, I would have left the job, too. Only because I began to see a special-ization in urban affairs, urban planning, and economics that I wanted to pursue and began to earn enough money to not be constantly looking toward my next paycheck, only as I saw my first jobs begin to mature into a career, it was only then I saw those early threads of work begin to weave together into a strand that would support me for all my decades in the field.

Perhaps those who left the field early could have found their own unique paths had they stayed longer. As the saying has it, much good work is lost for want of a little more. But I find it hard to fault those who step off the path of journalism early when what seems like a better life beckons them.

It took a long time for me to get to where I no longer needed the nightly bitch sessions in the local pub—longer, perhaps, than was good for me. But journalism is the sort of field one stays in only when the reality, however haltingly, however imperfectly, begins to match one's dreams.

*   *   *

The disconnect between the dedication of journalists in the trenches and the bottom-line orientation of the new owners was visible in Detroit as far back as late 1989, when the U.S. Supreme Court finally blessed the proposed joint operating agreement between my *Detroit Free Press* and the rival *Detroit News* after lengthy and bitter litigation. JOAs were an arrangement allowed under federal law for competing papers to combine their business operations—printing, circulation, advertising—while maintaining separate and competing newsrooms;

the idea was to keep a variety of editorial voices while allowing struggling newspapers to make a profit. The Detroit JOA had to overcome a variety of legal challenges, but after the Supreme Court approved the combination, Tony Ridder, the chairman and CEO of the Knight-Ridder newspaper chain that owned the *Free Press*, visited us in Detroit to talk about the new arrangement. We met in Room 100 at the old *Free Press* building, a ceremonious high-ceilinged space with paneled walls and murals of historic Detroit scenes looking down on us. Before a hundred or so of us from the newsroom, Ridder gave the speech that publishers and I suppose most corporate chiefs have been giving their troops for a hundred years. The new JOA that yoked the rival papers together for business purposes was a positive step, Ridder assured us. The outlook was bright. Our future was secure. When he asked for questions, there was a glum silence from all the journalists who saw the business combination as a surrender to corporate greed. Then John Lippert, our acerbic labor writer who had built Cadillacs on the line for GM before turning to journalism, spoke up. "Tony," he said, "if things are so great, why do we all feel so shitty?" The raucous hoots and laughter that greeted Lippert's question—and the perturbed look on Ridder's face—measured the distance between the corporate owners and those of us in the actual newsrooms. Let's not forget that this was back when newspapers were still, well, newspapers. We still had our full staff at the *Freep* of more than three hundred reporters, columnists, critics, photographers, editors, librarians, and assorted others. We hadn't heard of the internet yet, and it would be years before upstarts Google and Facebook began to destroy our business model. But even in that seemingly bountiful era for newspapers, Ridder and his rivals at Gannett Corporation, which then owned the *Detroit News*, thought their business model fell short and that they needed the joint operating agreement to correct it.

In the years since then, as newspaper revenues bled away to new online players, our corporate owners have tried multiple strategies to stanch the bleeding. Some worked, some didn't, and some are still in play. None of them have stopped the attrition in American newsrooms. The old economic model where advertising revenues yielded 20–30 percent profit margins was simply broken in an era of Craigslist and Facebook. The way newspapers had reaped profits for more than a hundred years was gone and was never coming back. But it's worth looking for a moment at what might replace it.

One now all-but-universal idea is the paywall, the tactic of charging readers to read stories in newspapers' online editions. A lot of the major publications—the *New York Times*, the *Wall Street Journal*, the *New Yorker*, the *Economist*—have created paywalls, as have a lot of smaller outlets around the nation. When a reader turns to those websites, they get to read either a small number of stories for free and then pay for more, usually by buying a subscription, or in some cases they can read only the first paragraph or two of any stories before paying up. These paywalls succeed as a business tactic when there is strong consumer demand for the product, as the *New York Times* has proven with its "metered paywall," which allows access to articles as long as the reader has not surpassed a set limit. After a sharp internal debate over whether to charge readers for online news, the *Times* instituted it in 2011. It succeeded beyond their dreams. The *Times's* unmatched standing as the nation's premier outlet for serious journalism gave it the ability to charge readers for content. Today the *Times* gets more revenue from online sources than from print, and their newsroom staff has expanded while so many other newspapers have had to lay off reporters.

In Detroit, the *Crain's Detroit Business* publication uses a paywall, and just in 2020 the *Free Press* and the *Detroit News* joined the throng, finally putting some of their best stories behind one. Before that, we journalists in the newsrooms had grown frustrated with the owners' failure to try the experiment. At least now the owners seemed to be responding, but we worried things were too far gone by that point to do much good.

Another tactic some newsrooms took was to cut back or eliminate the print edition and go all-digital. Many of our leading news outlets today were born as digital-only operations—*Axios*, *Politico*, *Buzz-Feed*, *HuffPost*, *Slate*, *Salon*—and some traditional newspaper operations have emulated them. In Michigan, the news operation known as MLive is the successor to a bevy of midsized papers around the state that are now mostly digital. The value of going all-digital comes in the savings of the cost of paper to print the news, the expense of trucks and gasoline to deliver the printed papers, the salaries for a large staff of delivery drivers, and more. When the *Free Press* and *Detroit News* decided several years ago to cease home delivery four days a week—they still print seven days a week but toss them on subscribers' doorsteps only on Thursday, Friday, and Sunday, when advertising is strongest—that move saved the papers some $70 million a year as we were told. Why pay for trucks, gasoline, and newsprint from Canadian paper mills when most people read their news online anyway?

Then, too, a new breed of nonprofit newsrooms is popping up around the nation, like Bridge Michigan in metro Detroit, an online operation staffed largely by reporter refugees from the *Free Press*, *Detroit News*, MLive, and others. It's a small but feisty outfit that gets support from foundations and reader donations. Even with its small staff of a dozen or so journalists, Bridge has produced award-winning work. There's now about a hundred of these nonprofit news outlets around the nation. They don't offer the depth and reach of a fully staffed major newspaper, but they often punch above their weight.

And traditional newspapers are looking in the crevices of American culture for new revenue. The *New York Times* now receives an "affiliate commission" when someone buys a movie ticket by clicking on a "Find Tickets" button at the bottom of the site's movie reviews.

And many traditional news organizations, including my *Free Press*, have turned to special events as new revenue sources. I was surprised when I learned that the annual Detroit marathon each October, sponsored by the *Free Press*, was a big moneymaker. (During 2020's Covid-19 health crisis, the newspaper scrubbed the actual marathon in favor of a virtual event but tried to get runners to roll over registration fees to the following year instead of refunding them, so valuable was the revenue to the paper.) The newspaper gets assistance from other sponsors as well, sells scads of t-shirts for the event, and charges entry fees for the full marathon of over $100 in a race that draws more than thirty thousand runners. Similarly, *Crain's Detroit Business* does especially well with its revenue-raising events; all its celebrations of "20 in their 20s" for young business leaders and the like generate revenue from tickets for the awards event plus advertising dollars from a special section printed to mark the occasion. Many of us in newsrooms like to scoff at these events as Journalism

Lite, something better left to the business-side marketing staffs. But if they save a few newsroom jobs, we'll take 'em.

The problem, of course, is that all these new stabs at revenue haven't saved newsroom jobs, or at least not many. Even as newspapers tried to mix and match their revenue streams—with paywalls, special events, special sections—the downsizing and layoffs have continued. I was fortunate to work for a unionized paper with a contract that had good severance language; the journalists we lost from the *Free Press* at least got some decent support when they were laid off or took a buyout. But the attrition hasn't stopped. During the coronavirus lockdown in 2020, the latest round of cutbacks had the Detroit papers furloughing journalists. It had become unimaginable that a *Free Press* newsroom staff that had shrunk from more than three hundred when I joined the paper to perhaps a hundred or less when I finally retired at the end of 2019 would ever restore those lost legions of journalists.

No wonder, then, that when corporate leaders visit newsrooms and talk optimistically about the future, John Lippert's probing question to CEO Ridder is never far from mind: "Tony, if things are so great, why do we all feel so shitty?"

13

Detroit and the Urban Dilemma

When I try to explain what happened to cities like Detroit and Pittsburgh and St. Louis, I usually put it in these terms: All cities spread out following World War II, thanks to the ever-increasing popularity of the privately owned car and the willingness of societies to bend and twist their whole civic life to accommodate it. All cities, freed by the car from the need to cluster tightly in walkable downtowns and nearby neighborhoods, began to ooze across the meadows and cornfields just beyond their borders in another of America's great migrations. At the same time, the innovative factories that powered the early twentieth century were growing obsolete, and manufacturing began to look away from the older cities to build new somewhere else, further depleting the urban tax base. This process of abandoning cities for suburbia dates at least to the 1950s, and as Thomas Sugrue's book *The Origins of the Urban Crisis* makes clear, the flight to the suburbs was heavily tinged with a racist reaction, in cities like Detroit, to the growing presence of Blacks in previously all-white neighborhoods. In America's heartland cities, those early postwar years were never the golden age of prosperity and well-being they are sometimes portrayed but rather saw a growing divide along racial lines that would come to define decades of city-suburban strife.

In the Sun Belt of the American South and Southwest, freshly sprung cities like Houston and Phoenix were encouraged by their state constitutions to annex their new suburban development, bringing it within their municipal borders and, thus, into their tax base. But all the older Northeast and Midwest cities—think Chicago,

Detroit, Cleveland, St. Louis, Pittsburgh, Boston, Baltimore, and many more—were barred from most suburban annexation and remained trapped behind their rigid municipal boundaries even as the jobs, the middle class, and the tax base fled to suburbia. American cities fit into two categories: the newer, "successful" cities of the Sun Belt and the dreary older cities in the heartland. Consider: In 1950, the city of Detroit and the city of Houston both measured roughly the same—139 square miles for Detroit and 150 square miles for Houston. In the 2020s, Detroit remained the same 139 square miles, while Houston had swelled to more than 600, thanks to its ability to gobble up its nearby suburbs. The comparison with Phoenix is even more dramatic. Phoenix measured just 17 square miles in 1950; by 2020 it had spread out to encompass more than 500 square miles.

This pattern has skewed perceptions of how cities are doing. Phoenix, the unofficial capital of the Southwest, would seem to rank light years ahead of Detroit in every category. But it's not so. While metropolitan Phoenix—the city and its suburbs in what the government calls its metropolitan statistical area (MSA)—boasts about 4.6 million residents today, and Detroit MSA (city and suburbs) is home to about a million fewer people, metro Detroit more than pulls its weight in economic terms. On a per capita basis, Detroit-area residents churn out $68,000 in annual output of goods and services compared to just $56,000 for those Phoenix-area folks (maybe it's too hot there to work hard!). Metropolitan Detroit also edges out metropolitan Houston ($64,000 output per capita) and metro Atlanta ($65,000 per capita) and barely trails metro Chicago ($70,000 per capita).

Such comparisons aside, there's no denying that the older *city* of Detroit, as distinct from its metropolitan region, suffered catastrophic losses due to suburbanization, as did so many other older cities. With a population that peaked in the 1950 census at 1.85 million, the Motor City saw people leaving by the hundreds of thousands every decade. By 2020, the city's population had dropped to about 640,000, the most severe loss in a landscape of older cities suffering their own woes.

By 1960 or so, civic leaders in the ailing cities began to react, mostly in dumb ways. Cities rammed expressways through still viable neighborhoods in the illogical belief that this would enable more people to flow into the city to live. Instead, as it turned out, it let them flee to the suburbs after work each day. Urban renewal, often race-based in its application, demolished more neighborhoods. And the process of deindustrialization, the shuttering of factories across the old industrial belt, cost more jobs and tax base. Racism and the race-based outcomes baked into nearly every aspect of American life made this process of suburbanization far uglier than it might have been. Many whites in suburban Detroit took to boasting they hadn't stepped within the city proper for decades and had no intention of doing so.

By the time I got to Detroit in the late 1980s, the urban crisis was already forty years in the making and far advanced. Yet cities continued, at least for a while longer, to continue to look in all the wrong places for solutions. Vanity projects like Detroit's Renaissance Center office and hotel complex on the Detroit River, festival marketplaces in downtowns that attracted vastly fewer patrons than suburban malls, budgetary tricks or raising taxes to overcome the dwindling municipal revenues—all these gave the appearance of action while doing little or nothing to solve the problems.

As I said earlier, German scholars coined the term "shrinking cities" to describe this worldwide phenomenon. There could be many reasons for shrinkage, all generally stemming from economic obsolescence of a local industry. Detroit's Big Three automakers, GM, Ford, and Chrysler, lost market share to foreign imports at first slowly and then in great gobs. As the auto plants closed and the white middle class fled to suburbia amid the city's racial unrest, Detroit's vast stock of wood-frame worker housing deteriorated. By the time I returned from the strike in 1997, Detroit's cityscape was marked by huge numbers of vacant lots and burned-out or abandoned properties. Many cities suffered something similar, but Detroit stood at the far end of the scale. With a population only one-third that of the city's peak years in the 1950s, Detroit was often said to resemble a man wearing a suit several sizes too large.

Comparisons with Dresden after the firebombing were common. For a time, there was talk of walling off some largely abandoned neighborhoods (that went nowhere). Once, visiting Philadelphia for research, I asked my guide to show me a truly distressed neighborhood. He took me to a district where rows of brick apartment buildings surrounded a park. To me, it looked like a solid urban neighborhood; as I wrote later, much of Philadelphia may be poor but the city still had good bones. Not so in Detroit, where much of the city existed as a sort of ghost landscape, with only one or two houses remaining on many blocks, where grass grew tall in the summer, streetlights did not work, and abandoned cars or even boats sagged on empty lots.

Yet we know that there are many chapters in the life of a city. As Detroit journalist Charlie LeDuff once quipped, Rome fell but a lot of people are walking around today in Italian shoes. Detroit had been many things since Cadillac beached his canoes on the shore of the strait (*Détroit*) in 1701—a French fur-trading outpost, farming community, shipping center for the Great Lakes trade, automotive capital. Surely another chapter could lie ahead, if only the leaders and tactics could be assembled.

So what *could* be done for my new home, and for cities like it? That's what I would set out to learn. And as I found my voice, I would benefit from working for a newspaper willing to give me a chance to use it.

14
Cities

A Recovery Begins

To many a viewer, the state of cities in the late '90s and early 2000s may have seemed as dismal as the fate of the newspaper industry. But new ideas, new ways of doing things, were beginning to pop up. These would create, if not a full-blown renaissance, at least the opening pages of a new chapter, and perhaps nowhere more so than in the city of Detroit.

In those years after I returned from the newspaper strike in 1997, Detroit was touching bottom. The population was sliding, employers were still leaving, and crime seemed rampant, at least in some parts of the city. The percentage of Detroiters in the workforce—holding jobs or actively looking for one—was under 50 percent, the lowest percentage of workforce participation of any major city. As I wrote earlier, whatever the metric—crime, school test scores, poverty rates, infant mortality, the number of vacant properties—Detroit seemed to sit alone at the extreme end. Even if its woes were part of a more general, national urban crisis, with wealthier suburbs ringing poorer and Blacker inner cities, Detroit stood out for its distress. Detroit, once the mighty industrial heart of the nation, had become the world's poster child of Rust Belt abandonment.

But things started to happen in the first decade of the 2000s that set Detroit on the path to recovery. Many of these trends happened off stage, out of the main headlines, and often nobody noticed amid the city's ongoing problems. But in my daily work covering the city I saw more and more encouraging signs. And these disparate elements would set the stage for what the world finally noticed was a remarkable urban turnaround.

Not far from where I lived on Detroit's east side, an installation known as Earthworks Urban Farm had grown on some former vacant lots. It had been established by a Catholic order of priests known as the Capuchins, who operated a community kitchen nearby, and the food from the farm made up much of the fare served to the homeless. The farm manager at that time, Patrick Crouch, showed me his spreadsheets keeping track of dozens of crops planted on a rotation basis, from tomatoes and strawberries to eggplant and squash. Beekeeping to produce honey was a sideline, there and elsewhere in Detroit. Meanwhile, on the city's far west side, the activist Malik Yakini had created D-Town Farm as part of an effort not only to feed people but to create a measure of restorative social justice for Black Detroiters. Elsewhere small community gardening plots were sprouting on vacant lots throughout the city, hundreds of them. One I wrote about was tended by prison inmates awaiting their release at a halfway house. I found it driving by one day; seeing a man working the beds I stopped to chat with him.

And the world began to notice. Many of us who fielded calls from out-of-towners coming to visit the city—artists, architects, urban planners, economists, academics of various stripes—used to be asked for a tour of the burned-out factories and homes, what Detroiters took to calling "ruin porn." But at some point, the visitors were asking to see the urban farms and other uses Detroiters were making of vacant and abandoned urban land. Late in that decade, the German Marshall Fund of the United States, with backing from the Kresge Foundation and other funders, created a program called Cities in Transition to take urban influencers from Detroit, Cleveland, Flint, and other U.S. cities to see what creative people were doing in the shrinking European cities. I went on two of these exploratory visits, to Leipzig, Germany, and Manchester, England, on the first one, and to Hamburg, Germany, on the second. And there I learned that reinventing vacant urban spaces was a matter of urgency everywhere, and that creative people in cities far and wide were looking to Detroit to lead by example. The repurposing of vacancy through urban farming and other strategies seemed to be what first gave Detroit the flavor of reinvention that would help create its emerging reputation as the Comeback City.

This effort was aided immeasurably by a change in approach at the region's many philanthropic foundations. Detroit, despite being one of the poorest cities in America, could boast a vast legacy wealth from the early success of the automotive industry. A lot of that wealth now resided in the upscale suburbs, but a lot also resided in the many foundations created during the city's glory years—the Ford Foundation, Community Foundation for Southeast Michigan, and many others. One in particular, the Kresge Foundation, founded on the wealth of the Kresge family's five-and-dime stores that grew into Kmart, led the way. Under its new leader Rip Rapson, who arrived in 2006, it began to reimagine how a foundation could impact a city. Instead of sitting back and passively writing checks for good causes, Rapson led Kresge to put not just dollars but staff time and expertise into leading recovery efforts across many fields, from urban farming to the arts to human services. And it poured money into high-profile activities. (Even before Rapson arrived, Kresge had gifted $50 million toward re-creating the city's derelict waterfront as the splendid new RiverWalk promenade.) The involvement of the many different foundations taking a more activist leadership role in Detroit provided both money and talent when the city's strapped municipal leadership could provide neither.

Another new tactic: So beset with problems had Detroit's city hall become that in the early 2000s the city began to spin off functions into a whole series of nonprofit conservancies, public authorities, and nonprofit corporations. Unlike the often disreputable practice of outsourcing public functions to profit-making companies, this spinning off of city operations in Detroit proved hugely successful. Two of Detroit's great public places, the RiverWalk and the central downtown Campus Martius Park, were built not by the city's underfunded parks and recreation department but by nonprofit conservancies. The city's beleaguered Eastern Market, the remnant of a farmers' market dating back decades, was restructured as the nonprofit Eastern Market Corporation in 2006 and, with cash from the Kresge Foundation, rebounded to become one of America's best public markets, visited by thousands of shoppers each market day. The city's convention center,

Cobo Hall (now Huntington Place), was handed off in 2009 to a regional public authority that immediately reversed years of decline and deferred maintenance. There were many other spinoffs—the city's historical museum, public lighting, workforce development agency, and others all slipped away from direct city control—not without controversy, of course, but ultimately ceded—and all flourished under their new nonprofit management structures.

Neighborhood nonprofits, the old block clubs that in many cases had grown into professionally staffed and funded community development organizations, did amazing work in neighborhoods where they were present. Most famously in Detroit, the nonprofit Midtown Detroit, Inc., led by the indefatigable Sue Mosey, led the turnaround in the city's Midtown area—the museum, university, and hospital district north of downtown—making it the most notable of Detroit's many revitalized districts. But there were many other successes attributable as well to the neighborhood activists.

And a new entrepreneurial spirit was sprouting. It was offering hope in a city whose signature auto industry with its vast workforces was a fading memory. Detroit's new startups took many forms, from new smartphone apps created by technology geeks to food production to bridal salons and bookstores and coffee shops and much more. I would write extensively about these startups in the *Free Press* and, later, in a book called *The Englishman and Detroit*. It chronicled the role of British entrepreneur Randal Charlton, who came to Detroit in 2000 and went on to lead the creation of an entrepreneurial ecosystem as director of the new TechTown startup incubator in Midtown. In early 2000, there was no such ecosystem, virtually no venture capital available to bankroll startups, no training programs for entrepreneurs, no incubators, no culture of risk-taking in what had been the ultimate corporate town. Beginning thereafter, Detroit began to see all of that necessary ecosystem growing and flourishing, and numerous refugees from the auto industry and other parts of corporate America began to try their hand at startups.

As a business writer focusing on urban redevelopment, all these trends became the stuff of my daily coverage. But by 2010 or so, most of the main elements of Detroit's recovery were in place. These would all hold lessons for other cities, and indeed were getting noticed from afar, even if in Detroit itself they were often overlooked as other crises loomed.

Perhaps not every other city could take advantage of these same tactics. Detroit, after all, had advantages, hard as it may be to think so. There was the legacy wealth held by the newly active foundations, and not all cities have that. Detroit had done exceptionally well with its series of municipal spinoffs, but there's no guarantee other cities would be so fortunate. Then, too, Detroit's rock-bottom reputation generated enough sympathy that eventually many people, in the Obama White House and elsewhere, wanted to help save the city once Detroit filed for municipal bankruptcy in 2013. And, as we'll see later, not every city that files for municipal bankruptcy can count on being as fortunate as Detroit was in its bankruptcy settlement in 2014. But at bottom, what other cities need comes down to a more elusive quality, which made all the difference in Detroit—a willingness to think anew and act anew.

If in Detroit these improvements were happening off stage, mostly out of the headlines, one reason is that Detroit was distracted by the mounting troubles of its young mayor, Kwame Kilpatrick.

Back when Kwame Kilpatrick occupied the mayor's mansion in Detroit (and not the federal prison cell he occupied later), his father, Bernard Kilpatrick, used to live in my building on Detroit's east side. Grandfather Bernard would babysit his son's kids and I frequently met Mayor Kilpatrick in the lobby as he was picking them up. He was always friendly toward me, although he knew me as a journalist, and showed little or none of the reserve that you might expect between elected official and a reporter who wrote frequently about him. But then his strong suit as mayor was moving real estate development projects through the city's bureaucracy, one of the few signs of hope in a dispirited city, and since I covered most of these stories, we usually met on friendly ground.

Like everyone in those first years of the Kilpatrick era in Detroit I found it impossible not to be impressed and heartened by the promise the young mayor exuded. Among much else, he had the knack of picking up on my line of questions in an interview and giving me the exact perfect quote for my stories. Maybe I should have been a little more skeptical of that ability, but at the time it was uncannily helpful, especially on deadline. And his public remarks before audiences could be eloquent, even moving. Once, with Tom Walsh, the *Free Press*'s business columnist then, I attended a ceremony to mark the end of renovations of Detroit's Renaissance Center that had become the world headquarters of General Motors. Kilpatrick's remarks to the assembled GM workers were so spot-on that Tom and I had to admit that one of the perks of our jobs was listening to Kwame Kilpatrick make a speech.

One of my colleagues, M. L. Elrick, warned me early on that Kilpatrick was a liar and a crook. I'm not sure how he saw through the performance so much earlier than the rest of us, but of course he was right. Elrick and Jim Schaefer would win a Pulitzer Prize for exposing the text message scandal that cost the mayor his job and sent him to jail. The federal prison term that followed came after a corruption conviction that further demoralized the already beleaguered city. But by then we were all aware of how much we had been lied to. Once, as rumors surfaced of the married Kilpatrick's dalliances with other women, I was part of a scrum of reporters who questioned him at a public event. Standing with his arm around his wife, Carlita, Kilpatrick told us he would never betray the mother of his children in that way. And of course he was lying. His philandering didn't send him to prison; public corruption and perjury did that. But his many unseemly betrayals—of his wife, his city, and of the promise he brought to the public stage—make his tenure a bad memory.

Another reason why the nascent improvements in Detroit got little notice was the implosion of the subprime mortgage market and the Great Recession of 2007–9. This economic collapse hit Detroit with the utmost severity; tens of thousands of Detroit homeowners slipped into foreclosure, with a catastrophic loss of family wealth and the further abandonment of many structures. Detroit was hardly alone in this misery; the subprime debacle plunged the nation into the most severe recession since the 1930s. But Detroiters, awash in foreclosure problems, could be forgiven for not noticing that operations like Eastern Market and the RiverWalk and the convention center were all doing well under new management, or that nonprofit neighborhood groups like Midtown Detroit, Inc., were growing increasingly skilled at bringing needed development to their districts.

Why did I find this all so fascinating? Going back to my college days in Chicago, I had always found cities so full of life, offering something for every imaginable taste, that I grew ever more absorbed by the urban scene. The novelist John O'Hara once said somewhere that he preferred cities to the countryside because he liked bookstores and shops and culture and anything that didn't make him feel ashamed to be a human being. The suburbs were safe but bland. Cities were challenging, to be sure, but alive with promise if only that promise could be realized.

And if some cities like Detroit still bled from a thousand wounds, if civic leaders still made far too many mistakes, if decades of turnaround efforts had yielded too little in results, none of that diminished my interest in the urban tableau. In Detroit and other cities I found a story commensurate with my interests and talent. I felt more than lucky to spend my days writing about a world I found endlessly fascinating.

15
Writing Books

Reporters all dream of writing books one day. A good number of us do. It's not easy for a daily journalist to produce a book, especially if you don't have the luxury of a book leave policy at your newspaper. Even so, during my years at the *Detroit Free Press*, several of my fellow reporters joined me in writing books. Hearing a little of how we did it may help others get there, too.

Like many reporters-turned-authors, my *Freep* colleagues who made the jump to book writing usually mined their beats for material. Mitch Albom, today a writing conglomerate with best-selling novels, plays, radio shows, and more to his credit, was still a sports columnist for the *Detroit Free Press* when he wrote his first two books, *Bo: Life, Laughs, and the Lessons of a College Football Legend*, about football coach Bo Schembechler, and *Fab Five: Basketball, Trash Talk, the American Dream*, a look at the five freshmen starters on the University of Michigan men's basketball team. Frank Bruni, later to gain fame as a columnist with the *New York Times*, drew on his experience with the *Freep* covering LGBT issues and AIDS to write his first book (coauthored with Elinor Burkett), *A Gospel of Shame: Children, Sexual Abuse, and the Catholic Church*, in 1993.

My own path was similar. In 1989 I wrote a profile of a high-energy real estate agent, Ralph Roberts, for the *Freep*'s Sunday magazine. Roberts, then in his early thirties, was gaining such notoriety for his "madman" work habits that *Time* magazine later dubbed him "America's Scariest Salesman." As a real estate agent, he sold hundreds of houses a year, and had sold homes at his own wedding and at his grandmother's funeral, noting that his grandma would be proud of him. I spent a long day with Roberts as he made his rounds of client meetings and house showings and wrote my profile. A few years later, during the newspaper strike of 1995, when I was off work and doing strike duty, Roberts called me. He had gotten some interest from the Harper's Business imprint to do a book on salesmanship. Harper's offered to set him up with a writer from New York, but Roberts preferred someone he knew, and we met for coffee in a diner to work out a deal. The resulting book blended salesmanship tips with Ralph's ebullient take on his own career. My job was to turn our interviews into prose and to capture his voice—not always the most grammatical but certainly a lively voice. I forget now what we intended to call the book but our editor in New York decided it for us, coming up with *Walk Like a Giant, Sell Like a Madman*. It and a sequel got me used to working on book-length projects. The money I made helped keep me in groceries during the newspaper strike.

Next step: I had nurtured an interest in architecture ever since my early Chicago days. Beginning in college at DePaul, I absorbed a lot of the culture surrounding Frank Lloyd Wright's classic homes in Oak Park and the muscular new skyscrapers going up in Chicago, including the John Hancock Tower and Sears Tower, briefly the world's tallest building (now called Willits Tower). A bit later, the novel *The Fountainhead*, whose hero was a Wright-like architect, had a brief vogue among City News Bureau reporters. (You might read Ayn Rand's riff on Wright when you're twenty-five and fall in love with it, but if you try it at fifty her wooden prose and far-right ideology can look ridiculous.) When I got to Detroit to cover development news, including all the new projects going up, it was a natural step to write about architecture, too. I pitched my bosses on letting me do an occasional column of architectural criticism, and the *Free Press*, being the sort of paper that encouraged our best ideas, immediately agreed. So from the late '80s on I could add architecture critic to my name.

The local architects appreciated having someone paying attention, and when their foundation decided to produce a guide to Detroit's best buildings, they asked me to help. Like many such projects, it was supposed to be a large group effort but devolved to just two of us, me and architect Eric Hill. The volume, *AIA Detroit: The American Institute of Architects Guide to Detroit Architecture*, contained more than four hundred entries matched with photos by the legendary architectural photographer Balthazar Korab. Wayne State University Press did its usual splendid design for the book, and even in the 2020s, long after its 2003 publication date, it remains popular and solidly useful.

Part of our research involved tapping the knowledge of Gordon Bugbee, a veteran professor of architecture at Lawrence Technological University in suburban Detroit. Bugbee seemingly knew not only design details but the social history of hundreds of major buildings. With him at the wheel, we would drive around from building to building, with Gordon regaling me with stories about each stop and me scribbling furiously in my notebook in the passenger seat. On these drives his knowledge just poured out of him. One Friday afternoon, after our latest tour, he asked if we could drive down a street called Windmill Pointe Drive in Grosse Pointe Park, near where he had grown up. As we stopped by the elegant homes bordering Lake St. Clair, Gordon reminisced softly about long-gone friends. He thanked me for the stop, saying, "It was good for the soul." He died in his sleep that weekend. Eric and I dedicated the book to our wives and to Gordon.

No sooner had the *AIA Detroit* guide come out than the architects foundation asked me to write the text for another volume to celebrate their 150th anniversary. Once again, I had the pleasure of working with photographer Korab. Hungarian by birth, he had escaped communist rule and made it to Detroit decades earlier to work for the great Eero Saarinen, who tapped his photography skills. Korab went on to become one of the architecture world's leading photographic interpreters. Our book, *Great Architecture of Michigan*, came out in 2008, once again from Wayne State University Press.

Kathy Wildfong, my editor at WSU Press, encouraged me to keep going. I needed little urging, book writing being perhaps my earliest childhood dream. But I wanted to turn now to Detroit's nascent recovery efforts. This would be different from all the other Detroit books on the market, which traced either the city's fabled rise (the founding by Cadillac, the saga of Henry Ford and the Model T) or the city's long, dismal fall from grace, a tale of racism, redlining, and abandonment. My book, *Reimagining Detroit: Strategies for Redefining an American City*, offered some answers to the pressing

question: Where does Detroit go from here? It looked at urban farming, the city's budding entrepreneurial ecosystem, greening strategies
including greenways and bike lanes, new governance models, and a
lot of other approaches just then getting a first look. Many of the
options I wrote about did indeed spark needed change, and Detroit
became an urban laboratory for other postindustrial cities around the
world. A writer from the *Huffington Post* listed *Reimagining Detroit*
among the best social and political books of 2010. My follow-up
book, titled *Revolution Detroit: Strategies for Urban Reinvention*, continued the tale.

By now, I'd had books more or less pouring out of me. In 2015
WSU Press published my *Yamasaki in Detroit: A Search for Serenity*,
a biography of the midcentury modernist architect Minoru Yamasaki. But I had my failures, too. There was a crime novel set during
a Detroit industrial labor dispute that called on some of my experiences from the newspaper strike of the mid-'90s; several publishers
looked it over and passed. And there were a couple of projects that
started around that time that took until around 2020 to come to fruition. All the while I was writing for the *Free Press* almost daily, doing
the occasional freelance article for other publications, and keeping up
a speaking schedule based on my books.

Since I was working full-time at the newspaper, I had to make
creative use of my time outside work. Mostly I wrote in the evenings
after dinner, plus on weekends. As in so many other areas of life, it
helped to have an understanding spouse. When I started writing
Reimagining Detroit, my wife, Sheu-Jane, told me I was off dish-
washing duty each evening after dinner to free up more writing time.
When I finished up that book, I quipped that I had to find another
one right away to see if I could get the same deal again.

And because my book-writing hours were limited by my daily job,
I had to make any interviews I did for the newspaper do double duty.
When collecting string, as we said in the newsroom, on some topic I
was writing about for both the newspaper and for my books, I would
save any extra quotes for my books once I had what I needed for the
daily story. Nothing was wasted.

I never felt there was any conflict in using my daily reporting this
way. No daily newspaper story could ever hold anywhere near the

detail that I could get into a book-length manuscript. And stylistically there is a world of difference between a daily newspaper report and a book-length project. One of my topics in *Reimagining Detroit* was urban farming—a trend that was growing exponentially in Detroit. My stories for the newspaper could never more than touch on some aspect of the subject—a resolution in City Council, say, or a profile of a new farm in the city's vacant and abandoned spaces that was taking root. My chapter in *Reimagining Detroit*, "Potential and Problems in Urban Agriculture," gave me the room to do much more—to explore the history of growing food inside cities, from Detroit Mayor Hazen Pingree's "potato patches" in the 1890s to the Victory Gardens of World War II, and to explore the economics of urban farming, which as I was writing were a long way from market viability. And my book gave me the freedom to write in a more personal way than I could in a typical newspaper story. Here's a sample from *Reimagining Detroit* where I talked about working in a community garden in our own neighborhood:

> And, lo, the earth proved fruitful, even our much abused Detroit dirt, from which I picked bits of glass and other debris along with the weeds. Everything sprouted in amazing variety and abundance. Once, as we bicycled past on a weekend, my wife stopped and picked a green onion. Handing the thick, fibrous stalk to me, she told me to try it, so I bit off a chunk. Fresh from the earth, it was unlike any onion I had ever tasted—pungent, full of flavor, almost too intense to eat raw. We pulled up a head of lettuce for our salad that evening. Tomatoes were ripening by late July, and I was harvesting carrots (rather short and stubby but still tasty) in August.

So, too, in my follow-up book, *Revolution Detroit*. In one chapter I told the story of how multiple City of Detroit operations were being spun off into new nonprofit conservancies and public authorities because the city itself was too broken, too dysfunctional, to manage them anymore. The city's convention center, its public farmers' market known as Eastern Market, its workforce development agency, the city's historical museum, all had been failing or declining when run by the bankrupt city but began to thrive once reorganized under these new management models. I became a major fan of them. But the process of converting them was difficult and fraught with political controversy. City Council only agreed to each of the spin-offs after long and bitter debate. In *Revolution Detroit*, I told the inside story of the transformation of Detroit's Eastern Market from a failing operation to one of the city's great attractions. I had written several stories about that switch for the newspaper, but never had the chance to write with the details and color that a book project allows. Here's a short bit from when the new nonprofit manager, Kate Beebe, and her team first entered the market offices to start work:

> So on Monday morning, July 31—the temperature and humidity both rising into the nineties that day—Beebe and her team showed up at the city's market headquarters to find that departing city employees had emptied the office. The place was cleaned out. All the records were gone—copies of leases with vendors, payrolls, purchasing and billing data, everything. The departing city workers had left only a huge pile of shredded documents. There wasn't even any air conditioning. (Jim) Sutherland looked around and said, "Oh, shit." And he called his wife to ask her to go to Target and buy him a bunch of golf shirts and shorts and underwear. "I was like, 'I'm not going to have time to do laundry. I'll just throw it in the car and we'll sweat it out.'"

That sort of writing may be routine in another setting, but daily newspaper reporters don't get to do it very often. One reason I enjoyed writing books was that the format freed me from the confines of daily conventions and exigencies.

I was writing, by the way, for anyone who had the time and inclination to give my books a try. A local professor pitching his own academic books once sneeringly dismissed rival books about Detroit as mere "perishable journalism." Naturally I differed with him. Academic writing, while packed with great research, too often reads dry as dust, written for a limited audience of specialists in the same field of research. I wanted my books to be *read*. Just as my favorite history books are those by people who wrote with style and flair for a general audience—Robert Caro, David McCullough, Edmund Morris, Francis Parkman, William Manchester—I wanted to write so that even readers who knew nothing of my topic might enjoy my books. The compliments that most moved me were those that said how enjoyable the book was; not necessarily how brilliant or innovative, but how readable and pleasurable it was.

Now, no one should take on the task of writing books for the money. Most books, maybe 99 percent of them, pay little or nothing for their authors. I made about $20,000 from my first book with Ralph Roberts because the advance was good (Roberts got a lot more), but that was my peak. If I made a few thousand dollars in royalties off any of my other books and a little more from speaking fees tied to them, I would deem that a good payout. Counting the time put into each project, I found that book writing, at least for me, paid less than minimum wage.

But rewards in personal satisfaction and public recognition more than made up for that. Becoming a book author raised my game, enhanced my standing in my city, got me in touch with my audience in a way daily journalism couldn't do. Book signings and similar events gave me a satisfaction that daily journalism, for all its rewards, couldn't match.

And if book writing is difficult, for many of us it is also inevitable. I have loved books since early childhood and always dreamed of one day writing my own. If anything had made me what I was—my family background or my Catholic schooling or my love of architecture—nothing shaped me more than my reading. I savored my favorite passages years after I first encountered them. A passage from Susan Orlean's *The Library Book* struck a chord with me: Althea Warren, head of the Los Angeles Public Library, said in a 1935 speech that book lovers "read as a drunkard drinks or as a bird sings or a cat sleeps or a dog responds to an invitation to go walking, not from conscience or training, but because they'd rather do it than anything else in the world."

That was me. If, entangled in the demands of daily journalism, I had started writing books later than I had imagined I would, I was immensely happy that I had finally gotten to it.

16

A City in
Bankruptcy

A newspaper does its best work in a crisis. In the decade after I returned to the *Free Press* from the strike, the city of Detroit's municipal government had been facing an ever-worsening fiscal crisis. The tax base continued to shrink and new taxes imposed over the years had only made more people leave. Repeated mayoral administrations had proven unwilling to make the hard choices to fix the city's budget. And health and pension costs were swelling to completely unmanageable levels. By 2013, it was clear something new had to be done.

No major city had ever filed for municipal bankruptcy. The federal bankruptcy law, such as it was, had huge gaps that would have to be resolved. City officials in Detroit were unanimously opposed to a state takeover, which loomed as the crisis worsened. But under a Republican governor and state legislature, that state takeover occurred in the person of a new emergency manager, in effect a municipal dictator with broad powers to reshape the city's budget and operation. Governor Rick Snyder in Lansing appointed a seasoned bankruptcy lawyer, Kevyn Orr, as Detroit's emergency manager in mid-2013.

As Orr took over Detroit's municipal government and steered the city toward a bankruptcy filing, the *Free Press* called us all into action. Any staffer in any department who could contribute even a mite to our coverage pitched in. On the business news side my colleague Nathan Bomey (later at *USA Today* and now at *Axios*) covered many of the day-to-day hearings in the U.S. Bankruptcy Court. My own reporting roamed across a range of players in the drama—Orr's team, business leaders, bankruptcy experts, many more. And Nathan and I were teamed early for one of the *Freep*'s best efforts during the bankruptcy, a long-form saga that looked at the fifty-year record of municipal mismanagement that led to the collapse.

Nathan and I made an interesting team. I was a good thirty years older than Nathan, and (from what he told me later) I served as something of a steadying influence during our work, especially during the craziness of writing and editing on deadline. But Nathan's tenacity was incredible. He spent weeks in the city's archives at the Detroit Public Library to compile a fifty-year database of the city's finances, a resource that proved invaluable as we documented our case of municipal mismanagement. I did something similar at the library with the records of the city's poorly run municipal pension funds. The writing and editing took weeks and included a line-by-line read-through in a conference room with all our top editors. We called our saga "How Detroit Went Broke" and it ran on September 15, 2013. Nathan crafted the powerful opening:

> Detroit is broke, but it didn't have to be. An in-depth Free Press analysis of the city's financial history back to the 1950s shows that its elected officials and others charged with managing its finances repeatedly failed—or refused—to make the tough economic and political decisions that might have saved the city from financial ruin.

And the first quotation, from one of my interviews, captured the city's failed strategy:

> "Detroit got into a trap of doing a lot of borrowing for cash flow purposes and then trying to figure out how to push costs (out) as much as possible," said Bettie Buss, a former city budget staffer who spent years analyzing city finances for the nonpartisan Citizens Research Council of Michigan. "That was the whole culture—how do we get what we want and not pay for it until tomorrow and tomorrow and tomorrow?"

It wasn't all mismanagement. We pointed out how the twin scourges of deindustrialization and suburbanization, worsened immeasurably by racism, had drained the city of people, jobs, and resources, as in so many other cities. But we were unsparing in reporting city hall's bungled responses to the ever-increasing crisis in city finances. And we surprised and no doubt angered a lot of readers with our upbeat assessment of the legacy of Mayor Coleman A. Young, Detroit's first Black mayor, whom many suburbanites blamed for all the city's problems:

> Serving from 1974–1994, Young was the most austere Detroit mayor since World War II, reducing the workforce, department budgets and debt during a particularly nasty national recession in the early 1980s. Young was the only Detroit mayor since 1950 to preside over a city with more income than debt, although he relied heavily on tax increases to pay for services.

And through a series of clever charts created by our graphics team, we illustrated the city's soaring debt levels. We showed how the city's tax base had shrunk nearly 80 percent in value since its peak in the late 1950s, even as surrounding communities had blossomed.

"How Detroit Went Broke" was powerful stuff, widely considered the definitive piece on what led to the bankruptcy, and it continues to be cited today.

I earned a couple of footnotes in the history of the bankruptcy case. One happened in early December 2013, a few months after the bankruptcy filing. I called U.S. Chief Judge Gerald Rosen in his chambers at the federal courthouse in Detroit to talk about the case. Rosen was serving as mediator in the case, doing his best to bring all sides together to reach agreement. Our conversation was off the record, meaning I couldn't quote him, but Rosen has since spoken publicly about our conversation and its content and written his own account of it, so I'm free to reveal the story here. As we spoke that day, Rosen described his concept of what he called the Art Trust. He was urging the leaders of local philanthropic foundations to donate a lot of money, probably hundreds of millions of dollars, to shore up the pensions of municipal retirees that otherwise would be slashed during the bankruptcy case. Rosen said a condition for this infusion of money would be the safeguarding of the priceless artwork at the Detroit Institute of Arts (DIA), so it would no longer be under threat of being sold off to satisfy the city's creditors. And this new money would free up funds for use elsewhere in the complicated bankruptcy. As Rosen explained his vision, I formed a mental picture of this overarching solution that touched so many different bases at once. Reaching for a way to summarize it, I said, "It sounds like . . . like a *grand bargain*." At the time, that phrase "grand bargain" had been in the news because President Barack Obama and House Speaker John Boehner had reached a similar grand bargain on the federal budget—a bargain that unfortunately had failed to garner enough support. Noting that, Rosen said he hoped *his* grand bargain worked better than that earlier one.

Back in the newsroom, I shared my conversation with Mark Stryker, a *Free Press* reporter who covered the arts scene and with whom I'd be writing up Rosen's idea. We used the term "grand bargain" in our story the next day and the phrase caught on. Soon even attorneys in the case were referring to the emerging deal as the Grand Bargain, especially after the state legislature, major corporations, and other players pitched in hundreds of millions more to smooth the deal. The *Free Press* in this instance not only covered the bankruptcy but contributed the phrase that came to capture the historic agreement.

And I made one other footnote contribution to the city's recovery. The morning our story ran about the Grand Bargain, I got a call from A. Paul Schaap, a retired life sciences entrepreneur and philanthropist, who lived in nearby Grosse Pointe Park. I knew Schaap and had written about him before when he had donated $20 million to Wayne State University's chemistry department. He had read the *Free Press* story about the emerging Grand Bargain and told me he wanted to do something extraordinary—donate $5 million to Rosen's fund.

"None of us want to see individual people hurt and lose pensions," Schaap told me on the phone. "I think if they have to sell one piece of art, it will so demoralize people in this metro area that we can't even imagine it." I called Judge Rosen's chambers, emphasized to his clerk that Paul Schaap was serious, and passed along his offer. Rosen and Schaap met for lunch the next day at the Detroit Athletic Club and Schaap's money became an early down payment on the city's recovery.

If "How Detroit Went Broke" had taken Nathan and me months to research and write, our bookend piece at the end of the bankruptcy case, "How Detroit Was Reborn," had to be done in mere days as the city emerged from bankruptcy in November 2014. Mark Stryker joined us to form a three-person team. We each worked with the sources we were most familiar with—Nathan with the many bankruptcy lawyers (Nathan's excellent book *Detroit Resurrected* tells that story in vivid detail), Mark with his sources in the art world, and me working the philanthropic foundations and other sources. We knew we wanted a thrilling narrative of how Detroit had gone from the imminent liquidation of the DIA and cancellation of retiree pensions to a settlement that protected all the art and most of the pensions, and placed the burden of cuts on Wall Street bond insurers. We wanted to capture the drama in individual scenes and dialogue. Some of that we already had in our notes; a lot more came in a frenzy of reporting. To cite one case: I first spoke with Mariam Noland, president of the Community Foundation of Southeast Michigan, about a dinner she hosted very early on for Judge Rosen, Darren Walker of the Ford Foundation, Alberto Ibargüen of the Knight Foundation, and a few others after Rosen had first suggested his Art Trust idea. I had Noland recall bits of dialogue as she remembered them; then I went back to the others to verify and check their own memories of what was said. Here's a typical scene as we crafted it for the story. It covered the period when foundations were deciding how much cash to put into Rosen's Grand Bargain:

> About the same time, the Knight Foundation board of trustees met at its headquarters in Miami. The Knight trustees, including Noland, wanted to help Detroit, where the Knight family had once owned the Free Press. CEO Ibargüen suggested a contribution of $20 million but was astonished that trustees thought he was too conservative.

Beverly Knight Olson, the late James Knight's daughter and the late Jack Knight's niece, had tears in her eyes as she addressed the board.

"Jack Knight loved Detroit, and the Detroit Free Press was his newspaper," she said. "I don't think 20 is enough." The trustees voted unanimously to give $30 million.

Ibargüen left the room and quickly called [Darren] Walker [of the Ford Foundation]. "Listen, you piker! I've upped the ante. I'm in for 30, so you guys had better cough up some more money."

"You are an inspiration to me, my friend," Walker said.

The long-form story was filled with insider details like that. As "How Detroit Went Broke" became the go-to account of how the city fell into its hole, this piece became the definitive story of how it clambered back out. And it had been done at a breakneck pace.

The governor's appointment of Kevyn Orr as the city's de facto dictator for eighteen months and all the moves he made during his tenure continue to evoke controversy even today. The haircut given to retiree pensions (it could have been a lot worse, many agreed) was bitterly contested; so, too, was the spinning off of control of the city's island park, Belle Isle, to the state's Department of Natural Resources, even if many agreed the state had the money to manage and maintain the park while the city did not; even the restrooms on Belle Isle had been padlocked because the city had no money to pay for janitors. But those tough moves, controversial as they were, formed just some of the steps that allowed Detroit to shed about $7 billion in municipal debt. That lifted a burden that allowed the city to emerge from bankruptcy with at least the hope of better serving its residents.

In the end, the bankruptcy did little or nothing to address the city's underlying challenges of poverty and joblessness. But the case did lance the long-standing financial abscesses that crippled city government. Our title "How Detroit Was Reborn" may have been too optimistic; better, perhaps, to call it "How Detroit Earned a Second Chance." Whether the city would take advantage of that chance to solve its multilayered problems was something we'd be asking for years to come.

17

An Aside

On Never Winning a Pulitzer

I once saw Neal Shine, the longtime editor of the *Free Press*, give an award for environmental work to Carl Levin, one of Michigan's United States senators. Shine was not only master of ceremonies that evening but a master at any and all ceremonies, adept at finding the right tone—informal, jocular, supportive—for any occasion. On this one, as he handed Levin the award, Shine joshed him, "Now, Carl, don't get a swelled head about this. Remember, there are more plaques than people in the world."

Indeed. Journalists are sometimes chided for handing out more awards to their own than any industry this side of Hollywood. Certainly I've won a bunch of awards myself, a few more noteworthy than others, but never did I take home the big one, the Pulitzer Prize. Nor, I'll add, did any but a handful of the many thousands of other journalists who peopled the profession during the years I worked. We journalists all fantasize about winning a Pulitzer, and the *Free Press* did in fact win it four times during my thirty-two years at the paper, twice for photography (David Turnley and Manny Crisostomo in back-to-back years), once for local reporting (Jim Schaefer and M. L. Elrick for exposing Mayor Kwame Kilpatrick's text messages, which led to his jailing for perjury), and once for commentary (Stephen Henderson for editorials on Detroit's municipal bankruptcy). Each year, if the *Free Press* happened to send in my work as an entry, I would get my hopes up; and when the judges bestowed the prizes on someone else, I would view the results with that slight disdain we all feel for something that eludes us.

But I did have what I'll call two near misses. In 1988, I was part of the three-person team at the *Free Press*, along with David Everett and Teresa Blossom, that produced our series "The Race for Money." We demonstrated that local banks had more or less systematically excluded Black residents of Detroit from mortgage loans, even in stable, middle-class neighborhoods in the city. We also looked at the banks' failure to support Detroit in other ways, whether by backing redevelopment projects or participating in government-supported loan programs for small businesses. The project ran big, created a stir in town, and prompted the banks into making a billion dollars in commitments for new lending in the city. It was the kind of big-impact project that normally would be up there as a favorite for a Pulitzer . . . except that reporter Bill Dedman at the Atlanta *Journal-Constitution* was doing something similar using mortgage data in his town, published his story a few weeks before we did ours, and he won the Pulitzer, not us. Timing, as they say, is everything.

Then, in 2013, we hoped that our "How Detroit Went Broke" project would win. When the *Free Press* sent in its entries for Pulitzers the next spring, we flooded the zone: Stephen Henderson for his thoughtful commentaries, the staff at large for breaking news coverage of the bankruptcy, Nathan and I for exploratory journalism for "How Detroit Went Broke," among other entries. Given how Detroit's bankruptcy had riveted the nation and that our coverage had been so thorough, we sensed we had a good shot at winning something. And the *Free Press* did snare a Pulitzer, but it was for Henderson's editorials, not for Nathan and me. As we gathered around Stephen to pop champagne and celebrate his win, he kindly said he thought "How Detroit Went Broke" was the best thing we had published that year. I was happy for Stephen, and my disappointment over not winning, while it smarted, faded as it always did.

The Pulitzers are a brief annual ritual where thousands of journalists allow themselves to dream again what F. Scott Fitzgerald once called their old best dreams. And then, as even the winners have learned, you still must go back to work the next morning. Winning prizes is fun, no doubt; but if the work itself is not reward enough, you're in the wrong business.

18
Union President

During the city's bankruptcy year I took on another role in addition to my reporting. Let me start the story this way:

Toward the end of my career with the *Detroit Free Press* I received a subpoena to appear for a deposition in a lawsuit. Several of my women colleagues in the *Free Press* newsroom were suing the owners of the newspaper over what they believed were unfair low pay rates for women. As president of the Newspaper Guild of Detroit I had spoken with most or all of the women about their concerns, and the attorneys wanted to depose me about that. A lot of the conversations I'd had with the women in the lawsuit were confidential union business so I couldn't share very much. But at one point, as a lawyer for the women took me through my background, she asked me, "Why did you want to be union president?"

My answer was spontaneous and heartfelt. It's right there in the transcript.

"I did *not* want to be union president," I said, and there were a few smiles in the room. Indeed, when the job was first suggested to me in early 2014, my initial reaction was to try to get out of it.

It came about like this: Lou Mleczko, a one-time reporter for the *Detroit News*, had been president of the Newspaper Guild of Detroit for thirty-eight years, surely one of the longest tenures on record. For the final twenty of those years, Mleczko also doubled as the guild's administrative officer, or A.O., the paid staffer of the union. Generally the positions of union president and A.O. are filled by different people; the president is the unpaid volunteer who still works in the newsroom as a journalist while the A.O. is the paid staffer, generally not a journalist, who files grievances on behalf of the members, collects dues, pays bills, and otherwise helps the president and other officers steer the ship.

Back in the 1960s or so, the Newspaper Guild of Detroit had about a thousand members. The guild represented not only the newsroom staffs of the *Free Press* and the *News* but some smaller publications and a lot of the publishers' business-side employees in advertising and other departments. Besides the A.O., the guild at that time employed secretarial help and maintained a suite of offices in a downtown skyscraper. Flush with dues revenues, the Detroit guild was even able to help lease a car for the A.O.

But those flush days were long gone by 2014. Cutbacks in the newsroom had trimmed our total membership ranks to about 250 over several units. We were soon to lose a couple of our smaller units, including the janitors who cleaned the building and the small staff of the *Michigan Catholic* when it ceased publication.

Lou Mleczko had run for his first term as president in 1976 and took over as A.O. during the newspaper strike in the mid-'90s. But he'd had a couple of heart procedures along the way and by 2014, when he was in his sixties, he decided it was time to retire. Lou met with me and asked me to run for president.

My first instinct was to duck it. I had been around union work long enough to know the president carried a pretty heavy load. Among other things, the president had the unenviable job of confronting our executive editor or publisher as the spokesman for the members and their complaints. I might have to consult with my boss as a journalist one minute about a story I was working on and the next minute tell him we were filing a grievance over some contract dispute. That could put me in an uncomfortable spot. Then, too, being the president meant being in lots of meetings—like everyone I hate meetings—and it meant being the one who supposedly had the answers (even if often there weren't any) for our concerns over the state of our industry. And beyond the workload and the need to confront my bosses on thorny issues, I had one fear that I kept hidden so deep that I never mentioned it to anyone: With newsroom losses mounting and the layoffs gutting our staff, I didn't want to be the guy who lost the union on his watch. The Newspaper Guild of

Detroit had endured proudly for more than seventy-five years. Would I be the one who fumbled it away? I feared that more than anything.

But as Mleczko and I talked, I came to see that if not me then someone *like me* should take the job. I checked a lot of the boxes: I was a longtime member of the guild. I had done shop-steward training. I had been through the 1995 strike. Since the late '90s I had been one of three guild trustees on our newsroom's pension plan. I had been part of the guild's bargaining team for the past few rounds of contract negotiations. Moreover, as a business journalist I was not afraid of numbers or spreadsheets or financial documents that would confront the new president. And I had read deeply in labor history, and I was a believer in the role of unions as the vehicle for empowerment of workers. Indeed, as I told my readers in my newspaper columns, I considered Walter Reuther, the legendary leader of the United Auto Workers, a personal hero. With my background and interests, the job description of guild president could almost have been written for me.

So I agreed to run with a couple of assurances from Lou. First, I would do just one two-year term. And second, if during that term I got a better job offer from another news organization I would be free to resign. Mleczko nodded, agreeing to all that. He probably recognized that I was one of those guys who hesitate even when finding a role we were born to play.

*   *   *

The actual election was a formality. Our Detroit guild hadn't had a contested election for officers in decades; whoever was dopey enough to volunteer got the jobs. In early 2014 I took over from Mleczko as president of the Newspaper Guild of Detroit.

There were immediate problems. Finding a new A.O. was one. Toward the end of his years in office Mleczko had hired a former reporter from Ohio named Lou Greco to take over that post. Greco had helped organize his paper in Dayton and was giving up journalism for full-time union work. I was one of the guild leaders to interview him and was happy to have him on board in Detroit. But it was clear he was bound for bigger things and within several months of my tenure he got a higher-level job as an organizer with the national news guild.

So almost right away I had to find someone new. A young woman named Stevie Blanchard, who worked part-time for the local AFL-CIO office, had attended a couple of our monthly meetings and avidly wanted a career in union work. She was just in her midtwenties and her only real qualification was her enthusiasm for the task. Often those are the best hires. We negotiated a contract, and she became our administrative officer and remains in that post today several years on.

Money, once no problem for the Detroit guild, was a real and growing concern by the time I took over. Our income came almost entirely from member dues. With layoffs and buyouts devastating our newsrooms, our dues revenue steadily declined. Working with Stevie Blanchard we cut expenses early and often. To save on rent we downsized our office from a roomy suite to a small, single-room office, and then reduced it yet again to a cubbyhole for Stevie in another union's offices. The office landline phone was gone in favor of a cheaper cell phone; ditto the desktop computer in favor of a laptop. We cut back our monthly visits from our bookkeeper to every other month, and trimmed everywhere else we could.

And here I came up with one of the ideas that did the most good during my tenure. Our long-term savings, which we called our strike fund or our war chest, had been sitting for many years in local savings accounts. There it was safe but earned next to nothing in interest. I knew we could do better if we were willing to accept a little more risk. So at my urging our board approved moving the total amount, then about $240,000, into a moderately aggressive stock-and-bond account with the local Merrill Lynch office. We hit the bull market at just the right time and within a couple of years had gained about $50,000 in the account. That went a long way toward ensuring that the guild would be able to continue its work without going broke.

Perhaps the most critical challenge was simply to get our members to engage more actively with their union. Lou Greco, when he came aboard as our new A.O., complained that the Detroit guild lacked a pulse—that we got everyone riled up at contract bargaining time but otherwise the members were quiescent. There was some justice in that. Our union had been in place for so long—and it had been a generation since the newspaper strike of '95 had run its course—that many members were content to let the leaders do the work and otherwise not bother them. Then, too, Lou Mleczko and his wife, Lorie, had run the guild office by themselves for so many years that others hadn't needed to step up. Their retirement left us with a dearth of leadership. With the future of the union in Detroit newsrooms on the line, we had to do better.

And so we did. Several journalists in our newsrooms stepped up to take on the other leadership roles of unit chairs and vice-chairs. We sent members to training sessions with the national guild. With rallies and t-shirts and emails and much more, we slowly got members more engaged with their union. When our next round of contract talks began in late 2015, continuing into early 2016, the membership had warmed to their task of vocal support.

That round of contract talks was difficult, as they always are. Among other challenges, Gannett, the owner of the *Free Press*, played hardball by not agreeing to an automatic extension of contract terms during negotiations once our contract expired in February 2016. That meant that the dues check-off, in which the company deducted our union dues from our paychecks and forwarded the money to the guild, would no longer happen. It was a tactic aimed at breaking the union's will by starving it of funds. Fortunately we reached a settlement before it did any long-term damage. But that wasn't the toughest issue that round.

Gannett, as a national newspaper chain, had been working for years to consolidate some operations in regional hubs. The *Free Press* was perhaps its last paper other than *USA Today* to have its own staff of copy editors. The company's lawyer demanded in bargaining that the guild agree to outsource our copy desk—affecting about twelve to fifteen loyal members and workers—to a regional hub in Louisville. Those losing their jobs in Detroit could apply for jobs in Louisville, but it was clear most would simply have to find something else to do. It was the most bitterly contested issue of that round of talks. We had successfully put off outsourcing in a previous round, but it seemed clear we would not be able to do so indefinitely. We negotiated the best deal we could: outsourcing would not begin for another eighteen months; those losing jobs would get extended severance of up to a full year's pay; there was a path to early retirement benefits for those nearing but not quite at the age to claim their pension. When we agreed to the deal, some in the newsroom accused guild leadership of selling out the copy editors; there was one particularly nasty shouting match. After extensive discussions and debate the membership did ratify the deal almost unanimously, although for some the bitterness lingered. As a teachers union leader told me once, sometimes being a union leader is less about making new gains than it is about managing the pain as best we can.

* * *

It was during that 2016 round of bargaining that the guild first raised the issue of pay levels for women in the newsrooms. We presented a data analysis of pay rates by seniority levels and assignments showing that women were consistently earning less than men in the newsroom with similar experience and assignments. Even raising the issue all but blew up the talks. There were angry recriminations across the table. To salvage a contract deal we agreed to pursue the issue further during the term of the new contract. We did, but with no resolution, and eventually several women on their own sued the company. A couple of the women settled out of court, another one was dismissed from the suit, and one was still pending as I write this. I wish we had been able to resolve the issue through negotiations, but sometimes it doesn't happen that way.

* * *

As guild president I got called into several disciplinary cases to represent our members. One Saturday afternoon I got a call at home from the company's human resources director. There was an issue with one of our members, who was in the office at that moment and facing discipline. Could I come in? I drove to the newspaper and found that the company had accused our member of using alcohol on the job. There also seemed to be some other underlying issues that were harder to get at. This member had a long and distinguished record and was blindsided by the accusations. The company was talking about suspending the member for a week without pay and issuing a final-warning letter, in which the next offense meant dismissal. The member and I got off by ourselves to talk; I have rarely seen a colleague so distraught, tearful, angry, and confused. I called the guild's lawyer, Duane Ice, and we went back and forth with the company's human resources man until I gradually talked our member down from the ledge of anger and confusion. In the end, we reached a good resolution. The company withdrew the week's suspension totally, reduced the final-warning letter to a mere reprimand, and told the member to take a few days' vacation to settle down. The member returned to work in a few days and there were no further accusations.

Several other personnel cases came up on my watch. We couldn't talk about these publicly since personnel matters are confidential. But this was one of our most important duties and a source of quiet satisfaction. In almost every case we handled during my tenure, the guild was able to ratchet back the discipline the company had initially imposed.

* * *

And so in this way my single two-year term evolved into three terms and six years at the helm of the Detroit guild. I stayed until it was time for me to retire from the paper, which I did at age seventy; I thought that was also a good time to turn over guild leadership to the ones who would carry the mission forward. Layoffs and buyouts had devastated our union during my six years in office; from around 250 members when I took over as president, we were down at the end to perhaps half that. But cutbacks weren't the whole story. We had a lot to be proud of. The Detroit guild remained a force in our newsrooms in the early 2020s, with a feisty membership, money in the bank, a solid A.O. in Stevie Blanchard, and a cadre of newsroom leaders taking on every issue that arose.

Best of all, our union had a pulse that beat loud enough to be heard even in the distant bastions of corporate ownership. Not a bad record, that.

19
Pension Trustee

In our household my wife keeps our checkbook, so you may not think I'd be the ideal person to manage a $100 million pension fund. But sometimes journalism and union work happen like that.

Not long after returning to the *Free Press* after the strike in the '90s, our Detroit guild president, Lou Mleczko, asked me to join the board of our pension plan as a guild trustee. The plan had long been in place and covered the reporters, photographers, copy editors, librarians, and other unionized workers in our *Free Press* newsroom. At that time the plan had about $60 million in assets held in a mix of stocks and bonds, out of which the plan paid retiree benefits and monthly expenses. Under the long-standing agreement between the union and the company, a board of trustees oversaw the plan. There were three guild trustees and three from the company. Since each side voted as a bloc it meant that all decisions had to be unanimous to take some action. Mleczko was a trustee for the guild, but there was another opening in the aftermath of the strike and Lou asked me to fill it.

Traditional pension plans like ours were once common throughout a unionized American workforce, especially in the manufacturing industries like steel and autos. They're becoming rare as union protections erode and companies dump their retirement obligations, shifting the risk to workers themselves. In America's woefully inadequate new retirement landscape, companies now offer "defined contribution" plans in which a company puts a fixed amount into a worker's IRA or 401(k) plan with no further responsibility. What happens then is up to the worker and the vagaries of the stock market. If an employee withdraws savings prematurely and can't pay it back, or if the market tanks and wipes out a retiree's nest egg, the consequences fall on the worker, not on the company.

From the standpoint of workers, it's much better to have a "defined benefit" plan like our *Free Press* pension system. In these traditional pensions, the plan pays retirees an amount each month for life based on a formula that takes in their years of service and their pay level. For someone who worked for many years at the *Free Press* at a decent salary, the pension formula might provide $20,000 to $40,000 a year in retirement, a very nice sum indeed when combined with private savings, part-time work, and Social Security. Those who were minimally "vested," that is, had worked at the *Freep* long enough to earn pension credits but who hadn't stayed very long at the paper, would get a lot less in retirement, maybe no more than a few hundred dollars a month. But overall the plan was one of the most cherished benefits of working at a union paper.

As a business writer I was familiar with all the basics of Wall Street and investment strategy, but still I found the intricacies of the various ways to invest our plan assets new territory. The complexity came in weighing the merits of large-cap versus small-cap funds, long-term versus short-term bonds, real estate investment trusts and multiasset class funds, learning how to benchmark our performance against various indices—and there's more. I learned why actuaries make so much money. The tangle of IRS regulations and conflicting ways of calculating our assets-to-liabilities ratio could leave me scratching my head even after years of trying to fathom them.

Fortunately we were a conservative bunch of trustees, both on the company and on the guild side. While the City of Detroit municipal retirement system in those years was riddled with bad investments and charges of corruption, our *Free Press* trustees never took crazy fliers on somebody's real estate boondoggle. We were invested strictly in highly rated stock and bond funds. And we had good advisers. I learned that investors with a lot of money, like our pension fund, got copious amounts of advice and analysis, much more than the average household investor might see. At home, my wife and I got our monthly statement on our retirement savings consisting of a few pages. At the pension fund, our quarterly meetings included a data dump of booklets a few inches thick of market performance and benchmarking against a range of indices and other pension funds.

Fortunately our pension fund did well. With a conservative strategy and wise professional advice we rode up the ascending slope of the rising bull market. Our plan assets swelled even as we paid retiree benefits and monthly expenses. And it was pleasant, after the long, acrimonious strike, to sit down with company trustees with whom we shared a common goal. Both guild and company trustees wanted the fund assets to grow as quickly as possible—the guild so our retirees' benefits would be secure, and the company so it wouldn't have to pump in millions of dollars to shore up a weak pension plan. Over the years, our plan assets grew to a high of $100 million or more, even with the occasional Wall Street bust and even as the demographic bulge of boomer retirements required more cash outlays. More important, with funding ratios near or above 100 percent of liabilities, we were among the safest and most secure pension plans in America.

Only as I neared my own retirement, by which time I was serving as chairman of the board of trustees, did the collegial atmosphere begin to erode. The company had always had local *Free Press* personnel managers serving as trustees; as the company consolidated its business-side tasks in regional hubs or in the Gannett corporate headquarters near Washington, the company trustees became corporate finance types who would fly in or participate by conference call. Even that worked okay for the most part, but in the 2019 round of contract talks the company proposed terminating the plan.

Plan termination could mean various things. It might mean freezing the pension credits earned by workers at their current level, with no more credits to be earned. That wouldn't impact current retirees, but younger workers would then be switched to a 401(k) defined contribution plan—less beneficial and riskier for the worker. Or termination could mean taking all the plan assets, that $100 million or so, to buy an annuity from a major insurance provider that would then pay monthly benefits, ending the company's involvement in our pension plan. The guild naturally objected to termination; the pension plan was a great benefit for our members, and we correctly saw the alternatives as riskier for workers. We intended to resist any effort to dilute our retirement benefits. There the matter stood as Gannett went through a complex takeover battle through much of 2019 (the corporation finally agreed to a deal with the Gatehouse chain late in the year) to be followed by the Covid-19 lockdown that put further contract talks on hold for a time. As I write this in 2024, our pension plan continues as it always did, but I remain watchful of any company proposals to weaken it.

The ultimate outlook for our *Free Press* pension plan represents the dilemma facing millions of American workers. Companies, aided and abetted by conservative politicians and judges since the 1980s, have succeeded in weakening union protections throughout the American workforce. Millions of workers and their families who once enjoyed good pay, health care coverage, and, yes, traditional pension plans are now pretty much on their own. The result of these changes is rising inequality, a weakened middle class, ever-increasing burdens on the poor and working class, and greed triumphant.

Our *Free Press* pension plan covers just several hundred current and future retirees and their families. But it's a reminder of the lost and threatened benefits of millions of American workers.

20
Negotiations

Back in my earliest union days at the Rochester *Democrat & Chronicle*, I saw that one reason it took us so long to win our first contract was our own ineptness. We were journalists, not professional negotiators; we had no formal union training, and we had too many members who simply wanted to vent their grudges with the company. Once, after a long planning session with our union president, Mike, I dropped him off for a meeting with the company. Mike was nothing if not hot-tempered. I had a hunch that his sit-down with the company might end in yet more recriminations. As I pulled up to the curb, I advised Mike to be tactical. "Fuck it," he said as he got out of my car. "I want to see 'em squirm."

I learned then, and I've seen the lesson illustrated many times since, that negotiating just to "see 'em squirm" is a lousy way to get a good contract. For one thing, it doesn't work. Management negotiators have the upper hand in contract talks. Newspaper companies, after all, own the bat, the ball, and the stadium. A corporation like Gannett has the deep reserves to ride out almost any labor discontent. This is especially true in contract talks when our union negotiators are going up against not just newsroom editors but corporate lawyers and professional bargainers. Take it from me as a veteran of multiple rounds of contract talks: corporate negotiators don't squirm. They may laugh at us, they may belittle our proposals and dismiss them out of hand, or they may get angry and hurl abuse at us from across the bargaining table. But do we ever have them squirming in discomfort at our brilliant sallies? No.

The other reason the "see 'em squirm" approach doesn't work is that it ignores the real goal: to get a good contract. Giving in to your feelings—venting at the bargaining table—is like a football player committing a flagrant foul just for the pleasure of roughing up his opponent, even if the resulting penalty he draws loses the game for his own side. Some players are happy with that trade-off. I'm not.

I've worked over the years with many union leaders but my main mentor in the intricacies of bargaining has been Duane Ice, the attorney for the Newspaper Guild of Detroit. Duane was representing the Detroit guild when I first got involved there in the late '80s and he's still doing it as I write this today in the 2020s. Duane would counsel us frequently that bargaining is like poker. You don't show your hand before it's time, meaning you don't react to company proposals, no matter how outrageous, with disdain or derision or anger or anything else. Keeping your poker face, you may ask a few questions to clarify, to probe here and there. Seated across the table from the company, you never let slip an unguarded remark like "I guess we could live with that" or "No way in hell will that fly." In the highly structured world of labor negotiations, such off-hand remarks can lead to problems. We might have ten people on our bargaining team at the table, but almost always Duane (or I as the union president) would be the only one speaking. As we mapped our tactics in advance, Duane would tell us that there is a time to pound the table and a time to be conciliatory, but each only if it advances us toward a contract settlement. It's like acting. As a union bargainer you do what it takes to get to a contract settlement.

Some of Hollywood's depictions of union negotiations are, of course, silly. In reality, while marathon twenty-four-hour bargaining sessions do occur, only brief periods of such a stretch find the rival teams from the union and the company seated across the table from each other. Almost all the time is spent in caucus, where each side's bargainers confer among themselves as to where to go next. Bargaining experts know that the real work of negotiations takes place in the caucuses, where the other side's proposals are analyzed and next steps mapped out.

At the *Free Press* and the *News* in Detroit, when contract time rolled around, bargaining would begin with a ritualized statement of goals and positions. In our talks in Detroit, Duane Ice would present our case why journalists at the *Free Press* and the *News* had sacrificed enough to save the company and that it was time to get something back. The company negotiator, a Gannett lawyer from headquarters in suburban Washington, DC, would talk about how perilous newspaper industry finances were and that any thought of significant raises was out of the question. These first steps usually took a couple of hours, to be followed by an adjournment until the next session a week or two or three later. As talks speeded up and the nonfinancial issues were settled—the question of pay raises always came last—the meetings would go longer and grow more intense. We worked under the maxim that nothing was settled until everything was settled. But in the end, if we were skillful and kept our heads, we could announce a tentative agreement and reach across the table for the ritual handshakes.

After we came back from the 1995 strike, I was part of the bargaining team for five successive negotiations. I've sometimes thought that the hard intellectual nut of bargaining could be accomplished in about three hours. It stretches out over three months because of the ritualized nature of the process. That process can be fascinating, and it can be maddening. But there's this: once the infamous mid-'90s labor dispute at the newspapers ended with new contracts, the guild and the company went on to negotiate several more contracts on schedule through 2016. (The Covid pandemic delayed 2019 negotiations, but even then, a settlement was reached eventually without a walkout.) It was never easy. Things sometimes got nasty. But there was no repeat of the strike, and the Newspaper Guild of Detroit remains in place and under contract today.

21

Columns and Flash Fiction

Despite our shrinking staffs and all the budget cutbacks and other worries that beset our newsroom, the *Free Press* continued to offer us many ways to do good work. Indeed, when people wondered how we could work under the stress of downsizing, we could say that it was the work itself that kept us sane and focused.

If I had one other career ambition remaining as I entered my sixties, it was to become a full-time columnist at the *Freep*. I had written columns of architecture criticism for a quarter century, numerous book reviews, occasional opinion pieces, but I still had never become one of the few full-time columnists. But when the *Freep*'s business columnist, Tom Walsh (the former business editor who had hired me in 1987), took a buyout, my editors tapped me for the role. I was on my way to Mackinac Island to cover the Detroit Chamber's annual policy conference when I saw the announcement in the *Freep* that I was now "Senior Business Columnist." I wasn't sure what they meant by "senior" as we didn't have a junior columnist, but I wasn't going to quibble.

If I came to my columnist role very late in my career, I tried to take full advantage of it. One source of satisfaction was to choose my own deep-dive projects. In April 2018 the *Free Press* published my lengthy investigation on the City of Detroit's neglect of its old City Airport, now known as the Coleman A. Young International Airport. The grand title, named for the city's first African American mayor, belied the shabby state of the airfield on Detroit's east side. All scheduled airline traffic had long since abandoned City Airport for the giant Detroit Metro Airport west of the city, and only private jets and small-plane enthusiasts used City Airport now. I had heard from aviation fans that the once-thriving airfield had been sadly neglected by a city government too broke and too dysfunctional to keep it up to date. And a tour showed me the airport indeed suffered from appalling neglect. Hangars were dilapidated, many unusable, and a once-thriving flight school was now a vacant eyesore. But how to tell that story? This is where some of the first lessons I had learned decades earlier at the old City News Bureau (which closed in 2005) helped.

I knew I needed certain things, or boxes that I had to fill, even if this project would be many, many times longer and more complex than those simple three-graph indictment stories I once dictated to the rewrite desk at City News. Among much else, I needed to uncover some killer examples that would illustrate the city's neglect. I had to find a counterexample of another municipal airport that was doing much better. I needed to explain why it mattered, and I needed quotes from a variety of people—pilots, the FAA, city officials, and more. Knowing all that helped organize my reporting and my writing.

Here's the lead of my story as it ran:

> The City of Detroit recently turned down a $4-million offer from private investors to build a modern terminal and hangars at the long-neglected Coleman A. Young International Airport as Mayor Mike Duggan's team raised the idea of closing the airfield permanently.
>
> The rejection of the offer from Avflight, the fixed-base operator at the east-side airfield still best known as Detroit City Airport, came amid complaints from airport advocates that the city is needlessly letting a potential asset deteriorate.
>
> Among other signs of neglect, the city hasn't staffed a Detroit Fire Department station on airport grounds for many years, which prevents some business aircraft from landing there because of insurance concerns. Nor has the city applied for a variety of multimillion-dollar federal and state grants that could help pay for needed upgrades to runways.
>
> The airport doesn't even have its own website, and the city does little or no marketing of the airfield.

All solid examples of the city's neglect. My counterexample proved to be the municipal airport in Jackson, Michigan, a facility which recently had undergone a $49 million expansion and upgrade paid for mostly by the federal government. And the story was studded with further examples of City Airport's woeful decline: half the small-plane hangars at City Airport were unusable; a derelict small plane had sat so long on the edge of the airfield that trees were growing up around it.

The reporting that goes into a piece like this takes time, and given our depleted staff at the *Free Press*, I got the freedom to produce a lengthy project like this only by juggling other stories and columns at the same time. So here my techniques for composing quickly, developed over many years (and which had earned me the reputation of a prolifically fast writer), helped enormously. Let me take a moment to explain some of those techniques in the hope that they help other journalists.

The reporting itself, the gathering of details, takes time, although it gets easier with experience. But only when you sit down to take your mass of facts and quotes and turn them into copy can you steal the march on less nimble writers. This comes after the dreaded moment when you open a new blank document and stare at it. It can be intimidating. Hemingway called the blank page the white bull. Writer's block is a real ailment. But there are ways to keep it in check, and the best way is to start putting words on the page.

In my practice I developed a habit to help me get started on a difficult piece. Once I have all my notes compiled (at one time in my reporter's notebook or on yellow legal pads, usually now in a separate Microsoft Word file), I'll begin to cut and paste bits that I know will be in my story into the blank story document. It doesn't matter at first where they'll go or in what order. I'm just trying to get words onto the page. Usually I start with the quotations. There may be a half-dozen or so "good quotes" that I'll want to use, even if I don't know where they'll wind up. I start to populate my blank story document with these quotable bits—cutting and pasting from my notes file into the new page. This helps me limber up the writing muscles.

So, too, with what at the *Free Press* we called the A-matter: bits of background or boilerplate that you know will be in there somewhere.

In writing about Detroit, I've often had to include a paragraph that went something like this: *Detroit's population peaked at 1.85 million in the 1950 census. By the 2010 census the population had shrunk to 713,000. Today it is estimated to be around 670,000.* I must have written that paragraph more or less that way a couple of dozen times over the years. And often I would put it into the story document before I knew where it would end up in the final draft.

Cutting and pasting this way, within minutes I could fill a blank story form with a bunch of good quotes, some A-matter, and maybe a stray fact or two. Working this way, I would soon have eight to ten inches of copy on the page, the writing sinews were loosened up, muscle memory taking over, and I'd be on my way.

And I also learned to mind my own internal "shot clock." In sports, players are required to take a shot or start a play within a fixed period. In NBA basketball it's twenty-four seconds; in men's college hoops it's thirty-five seconds. In NFL football, a quarterback must take the snap within forty seconds of the previous down. As Jeff Daniels's character in the TV show *The Newsroom* once quipped, baseball long had no such clock, so a pitcher could go out for a ham sandwich between throws—although the MLB has changed that, too. So what's this got to do with the task of writing publishable copy? A lot, I think.

When filling my blank story document with quotes and A-matter, I try to do it quickly. I don't paste in a single good quote and then sit back, mull that one for a while, go out for a latte, and eventually return to cut-and-paste another. Once I sit down to write, I try to get through this initial process as fast as I can. I get all my quotes and A-matter into my story document with virtually no time to rest in between. Granted, it's a slightly neurotic process, but it works. I can usually get the first ten or fifteen paragraphs into my story file in no more than five or ten minutes.

From that point, I find that transitions between the bits naturally suggest themselves. I write those. Ditto the longer bits of exposition that I'm clear about in my head but that can't just be lifted entirely from my notes. I start toying with those. My lead sentence or anecdote, if not already in hand, will begin to emerge. The same with the ending.

In this way, a first draft of even a moderately long newspaper story—say, fifty to a hundred inches—can be written in an hour or two. Granted, this process may not be the most creative way to write good prose. But at this point the idea is to defeat writer's block by blowing past it as quickly as possible, with the added bonus of making deadline.

Now, just as my reporting may take as long for me as for anyone, so, too, does the final draft, the self-editing and rewriting that are so crucial. If my first draft can emerge in less than an hour or a little more, my second, third, or fourth drafts may take much longer. Besides all the mundane checking of facts—Are the names spelled correctly? Is that date or dollar figure accurate?—I'm also checking for active versus passive verbs, eliminating adverbs and adjectives that weaken rather than strengthen a sentence, looking for all the little tweaks that make a story better. Paranoid about getting facts wrong, I'll often print out a story, take a pencil, circle every proper noun or fact, and check each of them again. It's painstaking, but it's necessary.

So although the initial reporting will get easier as you gain experience, don't expect to be able to cut away much time there. And the rewriting process to get to the final draft takes as long for me as for any careful writer. But that first draft? Blast through that. That's where you'll save a boatload of time. Your editors will think it's spooky. And your dinner will still be warm when you get home.

*   *   *

For some newspaper writers, turning to fiction is a natural step. Hemingway, of course, and playwright and screenwriter Ben Hecht come to mind. I tried fiction over the years but was never satisfied with the result. Perhaps my writing skills lend themselves best to nonfiction.

But occasionally a very short piece of fiction did emerge from my keyboard and even these stemmed from my fascination with Detroit and its urban prospect. One of these, published online at a site called Shotgun Honey, reflected the darkest days of Detroit's foreclosure crisis around 2010. It says something about the atmosphere in Detroit at the time.

Sinderella

Sam Danou slid into the plastic gloves he used to examine a crime scene. He didn't expect to find fingerprints in the chaotic swirl of a recently abandoned home. But he didn't want to cut himself on any of the jagged edges left behind by the metal thieves. Detroit scrappers came in two varieties, the careful ones who took their time with torches and saws to get a still-useable product—copper tubing, say—to sell to contractors who paid for materials in cash, and the dumb ones who pried or hammered out anything shiny regardless of its worth or how they ruined it in the process. This time, Sam saw, it was one of the dumb ones.

"Wonder these guys don't 'lectrocute themselves ripping out live wires," he said, poking gingerly at the tangle of connections sticking out of a hole where a switch plate had been.

"Or flood the place getting at the plumbing," his partner Elroy said.

"I know this street," Sam said. "Family that lived here moved out just last week."

"Foreclosure?"

"What else."

"Well," Elroy said, kicking at the empty soda cartons and fast-food wrappers that already littered the empty room, "it's the bank's own fault for kicking out people. How do they like their foreclosed property now?"

Sam took another long look around. He and Elroy were part of a new squad in burglary to catch the metal thieves that were destroying Detroit. Thieves ripped the guts out of still-good houses for pennies-on-the-dollar worth of scrap metal. Everybody knew the way to stop them was to crack down on the yards that bought the stuff from the junkies and home-less that brought it in. But so far lawmakers in Lansing hadn't passed the bills to let the cops go after them.

"Lunch," Elroy said.

"Get me a chicken shawarma," Sam said. "I'm going to bag some of this stuff."

With Elroy on the food run, Sam placed a few items in plastic evidence bags: a screwdriver left behind, one pink low-cut sneaker, a woolen ski hat.

Then he waited outside at the curb for Elroy to swing back around.

They pulled into the parking lot of an abandoned public school, slowly eating their sandwiches. They were almost done when Sam nodded toward a middle-aged woman pushing a shopping basket full of junk down the block.

"Pull over there," he said.

"Her?" Elroy said. "Shit, she's got ten bucks worth at most."

"That's okay. Let's go talk to her."

They pulled over just ahead of the woman. Sam stepped out of the car and said in a friendly voice, "Hey, Rosie, working early today?"

The woman, middle aged, shapeless inside her mélange of shirts and jackets and scarves, stared at him with a mix of fear and hostility. Then recognition flickered in her eyes.

"I know you," she muttered. "From Vice."

"Used to be," Sam said. "New gig now. Busting metal thieves." He placed a hand on the edge of the shopping cart filled with a gaggle of old faucets and pipes, soda cans, a lid from a pressure cooker, the twisted rim of a car headlight fixture.

"I found this stuff," the woman said. She pulled her outermost jacket a little tighter across her chest. "I didn't steal it."

"Hang here a minute," Sam said. Then, walking to the car, he told Elroy to pop the trunk. He reached in for something and then stepped back to the woman.

"You look like you could use this, Rosie," he said. "Too cold out to be walking barefoot, don't you think?" He handed her the low-cut pink sneaker.

A smile creased her face. "Oh, thank you, thank you," she said, taking it and slipping it on. It was a perfect match for the same low-cut pink sneaker on her other foot. "Where'd you find this?" she asked. "I hated to lose this."

Sam took her gently by the arm. "I'll tell you down at the precinct," he said.

* * *

I had been promoting Detroit's multiple greening strategies for some time in my stories and columns. In my 2010 book *Reimagining Detroit*, I urged many things that were later adopted: urban farming; road diets; spinning off municipal functions into nonprofit, conservancy-type organizations; removing an expressway or two to restore a more walkable urban cityscape. Did those things happen because I wrote about them? I doubt it, but I also don't doubt that my championing of these renewal strategies from a catbird seat like the pages of the *Free Press* got many people at least thinking about them. I spoke and wrote about these issues in an outpouring of stories and columns and, arguably, did so for longer than anyone else, in a city that needed to read and hear them more than most. Perhaps my journalism does, then, deserve some small share of credit for Detroit's comeback.

Occasionally, though, you get a little more direct feedback.

Even while reporting on these new recovery strategies, I continued to write the occasional architecture column. In these, I often urged the necessity for historic preservation of Detroit's stock of classic buildings from the nineteenth and early twentieth centuries. Through decades of neglect, Detroit had already lost countless buildings of historical or architectural significance; it was one reason why downtown Detroit was filled with so many surface parking lots. I and others fought to save the buildings we could, not just the true classics but the everyday warehouses and commercial buildings that, if renovated thoughtfully, could prove invaluable in creating the sort of walkable urban environment Detroit once had and badly needed again.

But in 2007 an unusual preservation controversy broke out. It wasn't in Detroit itself but in the staid Grosse Pointes to the east. And it wasn't about saving a neoclassical or Gothic structure but a wonderful work of midcentury modernism, the Grosse Pointe Central Library, designed by Hungarian-born master Marcel Breuer. Built in 1953, the library was considered too small by current needs, and the local library board members favored its demolition and replacement with something bigger.

But those with an eye for the best of modernism and the best of architecture could see what Breuer was doing. With its two-story wall of windows and its simple and elegant lines, it was unlike any of the colonial- and Tudor-inspired buildings nearby. Filled with natural light, the library symbolically opened its store of learning to the outside world and made culture more accessible. Demolition struck me as an awful idea. In my column I quoted William Hartman, an architect serving on the Grosse Pointe Farms Historic District Commission, who said the planned demolition would be an act of "cultural illiteracy."

And I concluded the column like this:

> Most new buildings in the Grosse Pointes get stitched together from architectural odds and ends—a gable here, a cornice there—in a sort of fake historical style. Commercial districts in parts of the Pointes now border on kitschy.
>
> Breuer's building is the real deal. Even if it's doomed, we can at least have a spirited debate about what's worth saving, in the Grosse Pointes and elsewhere. That could be Breuer's legacy to us.

To my surprise and delight, my column stopped the planned demolition, as library officials themselves acknowledged. With considerable grumbling about outsiders (i.e., me) interfering—one library board member told me the branch was just a shoebox with windows—the library board reluctantly began to consider alternatives. And Breuer's design, it seemed, had more support in the community once people thought about it. It took a very long time but in 2023 the library—with Breuer's building preserved and a sympathetic expansion added to the rear—reopened to the public.

People said I had saved the Grosse Pointe Central Library. If so, it was a rare tangible example of the good we journalists hope we're doing and, from time to time, might just accomplish.

22

Detroit

The Recovery

If I saw in my daily reporting shoots of hope sprouting up around the city, I was often alone in my optimism. In 2009 *Time* magazine ran a dispiriting cover story headlined "The Tragedy of Detroit" with a photo of one of the ruined auto plants on the cover. At the same time, the *Free Press* was well into the downsizing of our newsroom through the never-ending, demoralizing layoffs. The twin calamities besetting the city and journalism molded a public image of Detroit as a place at the end of the line, with abandon-hope-all-ye-who-enter-here posted at the city's borders, and with its journalists suffering one hammer blow after another. Not for nothing did late-night TV host Stephen Colbert open his interview with Stephen Henderson, then the *Free Press*'s Pulitzer-winning editorial director, with the snarky comment, "You live in Detroit and also work in the newspaper industry. Are you a glutton for punishment?"

But those of us who remained, both in the city's newsrooms and in the neighborhoods, took pride in the slogan Black entrepreneur Tommey Walker emblazoned on a line of fast-selling t-shirts: Detroit vs. Everybody. Another slogan I liked, in response to the idea that Detroit was wilderness ready to be reclaimed, was "Detroit Never Left." There were many such slogans, all capturing the resolve of Detroiters to fight back against the tides of history. In all my reporting years I have never felt that Detroiters were suffering from despair at the city's plight. Rather, they were mad as hell about it, ready to

162   JOHN GALLAGHER

do what was needed to overcome, and impatient for the rest of the world to see what they—what we—were really about.

I suspect many people date Detroit's comeback to the day in 2010 when billionaire businessman Dan Gilbert moved his company, Quicken Loans, from the suburbs to downtown Detroit. With great fanfare, the ebullient Gilbert challenged other suburban firms to do the same—*Who's coming with me?* And to doubters who questioned how he could make the move work at a reasonable cost he answered with typical confidence—*We'll figure it out!*

He did indeed. In the next few years Gilbert would buy or lease many of downtown's empty or half-empty skyscrapers, many of them classic art deco masterpieces from the 1920s but sadly neglected for years, and he proceeded to pour millions into first-rate renovations. He and his team curated a string of new retail openings in previously empty downtown storefronts, and they created from scratch European-style Christmas markets during the holiday season.

All cities have their philanthropists and corporate boosters—Detroit in its time had seen Henry Ford and his grandson Henry II, Alfred Taubman and Max Fisher, Roger Penske, and others contribute to Detroit. But no city anywhere to my knowledge saw a phenomenon like Gilbert's impact on downtown Detroit in such a short span of years.

Gilbert would go on to buy or control through master leases some one hundred properties in the immediate downtown, filling these empty or half-empty structures with his own employees after a series of superb renovations. He took over the long-empty site where the famous Hudson's department store once stood and began erecting what promises to be a major addition to the city's skyline. And he promoted a wealth of new restaurants and shops in the downtown core. Given his prominence as the nation's biggest mortgage lender and his ownership of the Cleveland Cavaliers basketball team, Gilbert enjoyed a national presence. His efforts in Detroit and the revival he led got many people, in the city and afar, talking about a Detroit comeback.

I covered all this from the *Free Press*. Like many journalists, I often decide whether I like the subject of my reporting simply based on whether they return my phone calls. Hollywood may portray journalists as scurrying down the mean streets and across war zones, but most of us are at the mercy of our telephone waiting for our calls to be answered. I often thought sourly that you could tell your relative level of importance in town by how quickly people got back to you.

Take the mayors of the various towns I worked in. In Chicago during my early years in the business, we City News Bureau kids were small fry, too small to get Mayor Richard J. Daley (Royko's "Great Dumpling") on the phone, although I did join the scrum at Daley's news conferences many times. When I got to the Rochester *Democrat & Chronicle* in 1978, I was surprised at how easy it was to get Rochester's mayor on the phone, but then my paper was the big gun in local journalism and harder to ignore. In Detroit at the *Free Press* in the late '80s, it was difficult to reach by-then reclusive Mayor Coleman A. Young on the phone, although I did sit down with him for interviews several times; his successors were somewhat easier to reach, the *Detroit Free Press* being too big a voice to slight, however much they wished to. I'm sure when the phone rings in the White House or the U.S. State Department there's a quick status check on who's calling and whether the caller is important enough to talk to. There's a pecking order, not just for institutions but for individual reporters, as to who gets their calls returned.

The same, of course, was true of the business leaders I wrote about. Getting a CEO of almost any standing on the phone means going through his or her public relations staff; these p.r. people often serve as a Praetorian guard protecting the boss, rather than as conduits of information whose job might be (judging from their title) to facilitate a reporter's interview. The bigger the company, the harder it is to routinely reach a CEO. *Free Press* auto reporters often interview the top executives in the industry like Mary Barra at General Motors and Bill Ford at Ford, but never without first negotiating with the p.r. staff. And reaching the self-made billionaires I covered over the years in metro Detroit's business world—Roger Penske, Mike Ilitch, Manuel (Matty) Moroun—could prove even more difficult. The billionaires tended to emerge into daylight only at carefully scripted events.

The sole exception to this was Dan Gilbert. I first met the future billionaire almost by chance not long after I arrived in Detroit. He was just a young lawyer turned real estate professional then, still in his late twenties, but he had made enough of a name to be invited to speak on a panel at the annual University of Michigan Real Estate Forum. I covered the event for the *Free Press* and was struck by how Gilbert spoke candidly about the abuses in the real estate world that led to the savings and loan debacle of the late '80s, a crash that cost the taxpayers many billions of dollars. In one deplorable case, Gilbert said, bankers in Houston had lent $20 million to a developer with no security other than vacant lots. It was crazy, he said. I was impressed enough with his candor to go up to him afterward and chat for a moment. He seemed happy to meet a reporter.

Jump ahead many years. In 2007 Gilbert announced he would move the headquarters of his company, Quicken Loans, from suburban office parks to a downtown Detroit location. By then Gilbert had built Quicken from the small startup it was in the '80s into a major mortgage lender, and he had bought the Cleveland Cavaliers basketball franchise not long before. He was a big name, and his move to downtown was a coup for a Detroit desperate for new corporate players. Once Gilbert finally made the move in 2010 (delayed for a couple of years by the Great Recession) he promptly went on his buying spree of downtown properties, filling them with his own people and with employees of other firms that began to join the relocation. From seventeen hundred Quicken employees he initially moved downtown in 2010, he grew his workforce to seventeen thousand in a few years. He became the name sponsor of the new downtown streetcar (the QLine) and promoted new attractions, from annual holiday markets to upscale clothing stores. These steps made him downtown's leading landlord and civic booster.

And during this period and throughout his time in Detroit, Gilbert seemed to be everywhere. He gave interviews all the time, appeared on panel discussions and at press announcements; he even took to calling or texting reporters like me when he was pleased or displeased over a story. It wasn't unusual to get a text after midnight, a trademark of his hyperactive style. An avid body builder of modest height, Gilbert was described in one profile in a national publication as a tight fist of a man, which captured not only his physique but also his intensity.

Far from being a scripted speaker like so many CEOs, Gilbert could be refreshingly off the cuff. His corny jokes were another trademark; at ribbon cuttings he often rambled far off script. He infamously wrote a hyperbolic letter that belittled superstar LeBron James in 2010 for jumping to the Miami Heat from his Cavs; it was the purest example of Gilbert's flash temper, but there were many others. His p.r. staff, all capable people, seemed to turn over more quickly than at many companies; Gilbert could not have been the easiest guy to work for, especially when those 2 a.m. phone calls interrupted someone's sleep.

Although a sophisticated investor and shrewd businessman, he was still a kid in many ways. Once his real estate firm, Bedrock, sponsored a charity event where for $1,000 a donor got to don harness and helmet and rappel down the side of one of his skyscrapers to the street level. Gilbert himself couldn't resist doing the stunt. Seeing the photograph of this billionaire and father of five going over the parapet on the roof of the skyscraper, I wondered if he had clued in either his wife or his insurance agent to what he was about to do.

Once Gilbert called me to complain about something I wrote. He gave me his cell phone number and told me to call him next time before I wrote anything similar. How many other billionaires give their personal cell number to journalists? Damn few. Over a quarter century or so of writing about Mike Ilitch's efforts in Detroit—he bought the Fox Theatre and built Comerica Park and Little Caesars Arena—I think I interviewed Ilitch on maybe half-a-dozen occasions. I sometimes talked to Gilbert a half-dozen times a month.

His many critics decried both his outsized influence on the downtown scene and his record as a mortgage lender. The federal government in 2015 sued Quicken for bad loans made during the Great Recession, but the federal case was weak and resolved before trial. All this I wrote about for the *Free Press*. At times I felt I was covering the Dan Gilbert beat and little else. But there was good reason. It's hard to disagree that in less than a decade Gilbert made a bigger impact on Detroit than any of the city's other business benefactors over many decades.

One of my roles at the *Free Press* was to prepare advance obituaries of a few major business figures to run as events warranted. These often sit in the files for years before we need them. My colleague Bill McGraw did an advance obit on Mike Ilitch at least a decade before Ilitch died in 2017. I wrote one on Gilbert after he suffered a serious stroke in mid-2019 at the too-young age of fifty-seven. He has been recovering thanks in no small part to his own iron will to get better. My advance obit of Gilbert sits there in the cloud against the possibility that the *Free Press* will one day need it. It is my sincerest hope that it doesn't have to run for many, many years to come.

* * *

Alternatively, many observers may trace the Detroit turnaround to the city's filing for municipal bankruptcy in 2013. The near-miraculous settlement of all bankruptcy issues by November 2014 put Detroit's municipal government on a good financial footing for the first time in decades.

And of course Michael Duggan, the former county prosecutor and recently head of the vast hospital complex known as the Detroit Medical Center, won election as mayor in 2013. Now midway through his third term in 2024, Duggan's reforms have done much to focus city hall's efforts on neighborhood turnarounds, on removal of blighted properties, and on promoting and nurturing neighborhood economic life.

All these things—the revived downtown scene with its dozens of new restaurants and shops, the unprecedented spin through bankruptcy in which the bondholders, not the citizens, took the big hit, the popular reforms of an activist and competent mayor—all these got noticed nationally. Not for nothing did a *New York Times* travel column in 2017 suggest that Detroit was now "the most exciting city in America." After his visit to the city columnist Reif Larsen told readers,

> In Detroit, the future is still being written. Time and time again I felt giddy with possibilities, informed in large part by the innovators I was talking to. . . .
>
> In Detroit—that fair city rising from the night sky—all dreams are possible.

There were many articles and commentaries along those lines, all agog with the good news from Detroit. Personally, having covered the city for a quarter century by this time, I was bemused by how the city's reputation had flipped almost overnight from poster child of the rust belt to the Comeback City. But to my mind, the 2010s, which saw Gilbert's work and Duggan's reforms and the municipal bankruptcy, was only when people *noticed* that a recovery was underway in Detroit. The actual hard work of bringing Detroit back had been underway for years before the bankruptcy case or before Gilbert came downtown with his thousands of employees.

Perhaps many of these changes took place off stage, out of the usual headlines that focused on politics and the biggest corporate moves. But I gravitated to these stories, and wrote countless articles and columns on them, the incremental efforts I talked about in chapter 14: urban farming; the success of the municipal spinoffs; new entrepreneurial efforts; and the city's adoption, after much debate and disagreement, of greening strategies that included the creation of bike lanes and new trails in place of old rights-of-way. The story of these moves collectively formed the core of my books *Reimagining Detroit* in 2010 and its follow-up *Revolution Detroit* in 2013. The headline-grabbers at the time may have been what General Motors and Ford were doing and who was running for governor. I was focusing on a range of creative people on the ground in Detroit and what they were doing to reinvent their city.

And along the way came milestones of recovery once thought unattainable. Both the long-dormant Book-Cadillac Hotel and the defunct Michigan Central Station stood for years as international symbols of Detroit's failure. Both those historic sites at times were recommended for demolition. But the Book-Cadillac reopened to fanfare in 2008 and Ford today is turning the train station into its future center of mobility research.

The work toward recovery has been long and tedious, beset by setbacks at every turn. Rebuilding a city built up over three hundred years means dealing with a legacy of debris just beneath the surface. When the Orleans Landing residential project of McCormack Baron Salazar started to dig foundations on the riverfront east of the

Renaissance Center a few years ago, crews uncovered sewer lines that, according to city maps, shouldn't have been there.

As another developer joked about his experience building a medical warehouse in Detroit, "We dug up everything but Jimmy Hoffa." Facing these and other challenges, almost every project takes longer than we think it should. When the Police Athletic League was planning what became the Willie Horton Field of Dreams at the site of the old Tiger Stadium, it discovered a regulation that a public playfield couldn't be landlocked by other development on all sides as was planned for the perimeter of the site. So lawyers had to work out a legally acceptable solution to keep the original design. It worked, but the process burned up several more weeks of time.

Or take mortgage lending. Detroit has been a city so financially broken that a normal mortgage market here almost didn't exist until just recently. Thousands of houses do change hands each year, but mostly through cash sales or land contracts, a financially risky way for a buyer to get a home. The dearth of market-rate mortgages reflects the legacy of racism and redlining that scarred Detroit and many other older urban centers at mid-twentieth century. But even bankers who admitted their past mistakes and tried to infuse more capital into the mortgage system here found that it was no simple matter. In Detroit, a potential buyer might have saved enough for a down payment but not enough for the repairs that would make a house move-in ready and eligible for a market-rate mortgage. Or an annual income that might support a mortgage in most cases might not be enough once student debt or child-care expenses were added to a borrower's burden. Low appraisals, lack of public transit for residents to get to jobs, food or housing insecurity—all these could hold back efforts to create a thriving mortgage market in the city. In one piece I quoted Janis Bowdler, president of the JPMorgan Chase Foundation, who told me, "As we've been sleeves rolled up, working in the community, we're learning over and over how multifaceted the challenge is. It's not just a supply of mortgage capital or a matter of producing enough credit-worthy borrowers. It's much more complex."

But slowly, even the fouled-up housing and mortgage market began to straighten out. Detroit's mortgage lenders, and civic and nonprofit leaders, have worked hard to overcome the challenges.

As they've counseled homebuyers and come up with innovative approaches to housing, the number of mortgage loans made in Detroit has been rising from just two hundred or so at the end of the Great Recession to more than two thousand in the early 2020s. Incomplete, yes, but nonetheless a sign that Detroit was figuring things out.

As I write this in 2023 and 2024, multiple construction cranes punctuate Detroit's skyline, and not just in the downtown and Mid-town districts. New housing and hotels are going up, new restaurants and other cultural amenities continue to open all over the city. Entrepreneurs by the hundreds are advancing their startups. The city's vibe is totally different today than the depressed urban scene I first saw in the late 1980s.

One recent weekend evening, driving from the city's New Center district after dinner the three miles or so along Woodward Avenue to downtown, we witnessed a vibrancy that was undeniable—crowds strolling on the sidewalks, new buildings going up, brilliantly lit shops and restaurants beckoning. And thinking of all those stories I had been writing for three decades and more about Detroit's recovery efforts, I mused, only half-jokingly, *my work here is done*.

* * *

I held my title of Senior Business Columnist for three years before finally retiring at the end of 2019. My editor, Randy Essex, gave me the whole front of the Sunday business page in the *Free Press* to write a farewell column. I used the space to reflect on what I had learned about my adopted city that for so many years had inspired my books and journalism.

I began that farewell column as I had my career in Detroit, by focusing on the long, sad half century of decline. But then I wrote about the many small recoveries that had inspired me. And I wrote that if problems facing Detroit and other cities were complex, so, too, are the solutions. Without question, the complexity of the problems and the difficulty of coordinating solutions made Detroit's efforts at recovery slow and tentative. But as I wrote in my valedictory to readers:

The good news—the really good news—is that Detroit in recent years has gotten so much better at working that magic. Whether it's city planners, the foundation staffs, bankers or neighborhood activists, more and more of these players have learned to reduce the barriers and make a complex system of investment work.

Does that system sometimes favor corporate interests to the detriment of ordinary Detroiters? Perhaps. Do we still sometimes see well-meaning efforts result in nothing much? Sure. Are there still problems that we have barely begun to touch? Certainly.

But the overall impact of Detroit's recovery efforts—efforts by thousands of committed people working across a broad range of activities, from workforce training to urban farming to education and transit, these efforts have slowly inched Detroit forward. And the city is better for it.

There's a saying that "nothing works but everything might." It means that there is no silver-bullet solution to our problems. But if we work across a hundred different fields, making progress in each one, those efforts will add up to something greater than the sum of the parts. That's the approach Detroit has taken and must continue to take.

There's a story from the American Civil War that I like. A new regiment came up to the battlefront and its colonel asked the general commanding where they should go in. "Why, go in anywhere," the general replied. "There is lovely fighting all along the line."

And so in Detroit. If you want a to-do list to take away from this column, work on whatever holds your interest. We need progress on public safety and education, but we also need to work on transit and child care and vacant buildings and entrepreneurship and any of a hundred other fields. Take your pick, and get busy.

It's a long and difficult task. But that shouldn't faze a city with a gritty work ethic like Detroit's. Detroit's story is so varied, with so much conflicting evidence of progress or lack of it, that even today one can lean toward either optimism or despair.

I choose hope. I believe with Dr. King that the arc of the moral universe is long but that it bends toward justice. And I hold with the message of Irish poet Seamus Heaney whose words about his homeland echo for me in Detroit:

History says, don't hope
On this side of the grave.
But then, once in a lifetime
The longed-for tidal wave
Of justice can rise up,
And hope and history rhyme.

23

When It's Time to Move On

A memoir is a public appearance, and one is inclined to stand straighter and present the best profile. Mitigating this tendency, there are no deeds of personal daring to relate, and no action of mine affected the battle one way or the other. This is personally regrettable, but it also lessens the self-consciousness of narrating in the first person. I was there; I endured.

—Charles Cawthon, "St. Lo"

For some reason, nobody ever asks me what I consider my favorite story of all time. But if they did, I might mention a profile I wrote back in 1991 of a Detroit-area businessman named Bill Davidson. I like it in part because it illustrates the conflicting emotions a journalist goes through on a big story. There is the initial enthusiasm that gives way to despair at the black hole of research and, later, to frustration during the writing and editing. There's the anxiety in the hours before it publishes and the giddiness you feel when you hold the final product in your hand. And finally, if you're lucky, there's the quiet satisfaction that stays with you because something you wrote turned out well.

The Davidson profile happened like this: In 1991 I did a three-month rotation as a staff writer with the *Detroit Free Press Magazine*. The publication was a survivor of that once-thriving but quickly vanishing breed of colorful Sunday morning newspaper magazines. During my stint I pitched and got approval to work on a long-form profile of Davidson, the billionaire businessman who owned the Detroit Pistons basketball team as well as the arena they played in, the Palace of Auburn Hills. Davidson enjoyed a public persona of a benevolent philanthropist and sports junkie who ran one of the best programs in pro sports; he was among the first to have his own private jet, Roundball One, for his players and coaches, and the Palace was the first arena to move the luxury suites out of the rafters down much closer to the action, an innovative and widely imitated design feature in other arenas to come. But Davidson's grandfatherly good-guy image belied some piratical business practices. Owning and running his Guardian Glass company, he had paid tens of millions of dollars in fines and settlements for stealing his competitors' patents, for screwing a partner out of what he was promised, and for breaking the union at his glass company. My profile of him exposed all of this, and the topper was the title: since the Pistons were known as the Bad Boys for their sharp-elbowed defensive play, we called the story "The Baddest Boy." Davidson and his people hated the story, and it generated a great deal of reaction, of which my favorite was a call from Bob Talbert, the legendary *Free Press* people columnist, who told me it was the "only *honest* story" that had ever been written on Davidson in this town. All reporters should be lucky enough to get a compliment like that.

What you've been reading in these pages was my life for the better part of forty years. Looking through my stacks and stacks of clippings I see stories I wrote that I had forgotten, stories tossed off on deadline and long-form stories that took months and won awards, book reviews and columns of criticism and interviews with the famous and obscure. We journalists like to see ourselves portrayed as trench-coated adventurers, but ours is a life spent at the keyboard, putting words on paper and now on the digital screen. It's okay to think of ourselves as social critics or political analysts or science interpreters or whatever, but at bottom we are *writers*. A busy day of chasing after stories always ends with putting words on the page.

The life of a journalist was made for someone like that young lad I was who loved books and reading but was too restless and curious to do anything but get out into the world and explore. Long after many of my early colleagues had given up journalism to go to law school or to snare a lucrative public relations job, I stayed with it. I cherished the byline and the chance to, as Mark Twain said, go all over town and ask all sorts of people all sorts of questions and write up the results.

But at some point, as 2020 approached, I knew my role as a daily journalist would give way to something else. With buyouts at the *Free Press* becoming an annual ritual, and with the severance terms in our guild contract still fairly good, many of us more senior writers were timing our departures to suit us. I finally took the buyout at the end of 2019. I had turned seventy a month before (my goal was to work full-time to seventy and part-time for as long as I wanted after that). My third two-year term as guild president would conclude in early 2020, and I sensed it was wise to give the next group of union leaders a chance to take over without me looking over their shoulders. Both of those made it a good time to transition to something new.

And then there was a lot I wanted to do that I couldn't do as a working journalist. I've always wanted to get involved in our civic life in ways journalists cannot; during my career I never once donated to a candidate or otherwise got involved in a political campaign. I could engage in those ways once I retired, and what promised to be the fractious 2020 campaign season looked like the time to do it. And there were books to write that required more time than a full-time journalist could give to them. There were new fields to explore like podcasting.

My family has been blessed with long life; my father made it to ninety-nine and my mother into her nineties. But if I had lots of years ahead, I knew I didn't have *unlimited* time. If I wanted to do some of those other things, to visit the cities I'd yet to visit and read the books I'd been putting aside for years, I better get to it.

It helped that I still cherished my role as a columnist at the *Free Press* when I moved on from daily journalism. As they say, quitting while ahead isn't the same as quitting. I left daily journalism because of the promise ahead, not because of problems behind.

But perhaps one never really leaves. I still say "we" when referring to the *Detroit Free Press*. And I still call myself a journalist because my mix of book writing and freelance scribbling is best described as journalism, although I now add "freelance" to my title out of deference to my friends and colleagues still in the trenches at the newspaper.

I found I slept an extra hour each night once I gave up full-time work; I had more time to exercise, and I definitely felt less stressed. But one doesn't so easily give up the habits of a lifetime. I was "retired" only for a few months when my editor from the *Free Press*, Peter Bhatia, asked if I'd contribute a new piece on the economic crisis due to the coronavirus pandemic. I slipped so easily back into harness it was as if I had never left, even if just for the occasional assignment.

Perhaps there is no one single story that's my favorite of all the thousands I wrote. Better to say I enjoyed my life at the keyboard and the give-and-take of daily journalism. If I've long since given up running into burning buildings to get a story, my curiosity about the world remains as fresh today in my early seventies as it was when I first walked into the newsroom of the City News Bureau of Chicago all those years ago. Every morning now when I go to the keyboard my work starts anew.

About the Author

JOHN GALLAGHER is a veteran journalist, author, and authority on urban affairs, particularly relating to Rust Belt cities. Educated at DePaul University in Chicago and Columbia University in New York, he joined the *Detroit Free Press* in 1987 as an urban affairs writer and continued reporting there for thirty-two years. A resident of Detroit, Gallagher continues to work as a public speaker, author, and freelance journalist.

Photo Credit: Nic Antaya

More books by John Gallagher and Wayne State University Press

*Yamasaki in Detroit:
A Search for Serenity*

*Revolution Detroit:
Strategies for Urban
Reinvention*

*Reimagining Detroit:
Opportunities for Redefining
an American City*

*Great Architecture
of Michigan*

*AIA Detroit: The American
Institute of Architects Guide
to Detroit Architecture*

Visit wsupress.wayne.edu for more information and to order.